Aɪ:
ANGEL
INTERVENTION

Compiled and Edited by

Ruth Rendely

Seraphim Alliance

AI: Angel Intervention

Compiled and Edited by Ruth Rendely

Published by Seraphim Alliance

First Edition

Library of Congress Cataloging-in-Publication Data

Softcover ISBN: 978-1-4218-3704-8

Previous Volume of Short Stories

When Angels Make House Calls
(c. 2018)

Table of Contents

Introduction

This is the second volume of short stories based upon the triennial Seraphic Prize of short stories that began in 2017. The previous edition was limited to the writings of Seraphim Blueprint practitioners and Teachers. For the 2020 Seraphic Prize we invited worldwide participation. Thus, the contributions in this volume reflect this broader participation.

I find it interesting that the death of loved ones is the subject of many of the submissions to the Seraphic Prize contest, both this time and last time. This may be because the heightened emotions associated with witnessing the experience of dying are so underplayed in our culture at large, and the details of such an experience are so memorable, that when they occur to us personally, it becomes something we wish to record for ourselves and others.

With the recent worldwide lockdowns and limits on Western democratic traditions, the Seraphim and other angels are emphasizing the struggle between good and evil in a more muscular way, and thus, the theme of this volume's cover showing that angels can mean business too.

Ruth Rendely Chairperson,
Seraphim Blueprint
July 2021

The Seraph Appeared to Me

It is 9:40 a.m. and very cold in the damp basement bedroom of my husband's goddaughter's home. My husband and I are packing to leave Montana after having traveled here from a two-week spiritual retreat at Mt. Shasta. I was more than ready to be back home in the sunshine at sea level. This trip was intended to be a teaching trip because I was scheduled and booked to teach a weekend class in Helena. News of our Montana layover turned our generally stable goddaughter into a hysterically emotional woman with a full-blown temper tantrum. Her explosive reaction to our trip to Montana, the part that had us teaching three days and visiting her for three days, resulted in my husband feeling compelled to agree to extend our visit with her to almost two weeks. I should have recognized the outburst; after all, I was raised by an alcoholic. But it wasn't crystal clear until I was staying in her home.

His goddaughter is a successful professional with a stay-at-home husband and two beautiful children, Ethan age four, and Caroline not yet two years old. This goddaughter seems to have it all: a fabulous home, a great career, money, and the ideal family. What I hoped to be a joyous time together was instead a peek inside the horror of alcohol abuse. The irrational, dramatic, emotional outbursts along with the focus on parties with friends and neighbors left the children alone and ignored too much of the time. I feel saddened to see the obvious signs of alcohol abuse and its everlasting effects.

In Mt. Shasta, we meditated with the masters, communed with the angels, hiked the mountains and the meadows, and activated our Seraphim Blueprint energies: two weeks of the most magical times of my life. With this high vibratory rate, my ever-refining etheric senses peaked. We flew to Montana to teach a spiritual healing class. The students were receptive, and the healings they experienced were life changing. All was in Divine flow, as we know it always is.

With the Seraphim grid in place, I slept in the basement bedroom of our goddaughter's house with my husband and faithfully practiced my meditation. I activated my energies and gave appreciation while praying for this family that has such potential for a bright and happy future: *potential*. Everyone gets to play at life in their own way. I am not to judge.

Finally, it is our last morning here, and our limo was to pick us up at 11:00 A.M. to deliver us to the airport. I am keenly aware of the life these babies are subjected to. I have a pretty good idea of what is in store for them. I don't want to go to that place of sorrow. I know I have plenty of time to meditate and run an energy. I know this is the best I can do right now. When I became a mother myself and felt completely inadequate, I remembered the Knowing Voice (God) telling me: "*Your only responsibility is to pray for her every day.*"

My mind floats across the events of the past month— away from home, my heart opens to Spirit. I begin, as I often do, with the mantra suggested by Deepak Chopra:

Who am I?

Why am I here?

What is my Purpose?

How can I help?

How can I heal?

How can I serve?

As I silently chant this mantra, I can hear the little ones outside playing. It's a sunny, warm, fall day. I take this interruption to mean that I should finish now and go outside and savor the experience with these sweet children before we leave. I stand up from my meditation position, and the moment I do, I hear an audible voice *"Get down on your knees."*

Instantly, I drop to my knees and close my eyes. I'm instructed to activate Seraphim Grace Energy.

I don't question it.

As the energy began, I suddenly see the Seraph for the first time. He appeared to me, and He is bigger than life. I can clearly see the expression on His face and the size, stature and magnitude of His being. There are no words to describe the energy around him. I now understand why people have described it as wings. I am shaking and crying with awe at the sight of His magnificent presence. I am crying uncontrollably, not because I am frightened or sad, but because the power of His presence is so overwhelming—stunning. I have never seen anything like this. I am not one that typically "sees". My spiritual gifts are those of "sensing", "knowing", "feeling" and "hearing". But now, I physically see this magnificent Seraph before me.

I realize He is too big to be in the room; he is in the sky outside. He appears to fill the entire section of the sky above the house. I have no thought. I am only experiencing.

The visual, the intensity and power is all I can take in. No thought, only strong emotion: love. Love is pouring into me, flooding me with gratitude and appreciation.

Only seconds earlier, my heart was crying for these sweet babies and the life they are subjected to and, in an instant, with the activation of Seraphim Grace Energy, I become aware of the presence of the Seraph, and sadness instantly transforms through love to faith and trust. My tears become uncontrollable because my heart is filled with raw, intense, unequivocal love, the kind of love that knows no judgment or desire for anything more than what is. This, I know, is grace being poured onto me.

I have no sense of time. I stay on my knees, allowing the experience to transform me. I don't want to move, I don't want this to end—ever....

Eventually, my husband came downstairs into the room to get me. I got off my knees and followed him outside. I did not tell him what I had just experienced because I did not want to dissipate the energy, or have anyone question me about the details, or take me into an analytical assessment.

All I knew was that when I was hurting, the Seraph appeared before me and showed himself to me; and when that happened, all I could feel is Love.

I stepped onto the driveway and looked up into the bright blue sky where, just moments before, I had seen the magnificent Seraph in my minds-eye. And to my surprise and awe,

He was still there!

Just above the garage, the Seraph was floating in the sky over the property. It was an incredible sight! Tears instantly welled up in my eyes, and I began crying from the emotion I felt in His presence. My husband told me later that everyone thought I was crying because I was leaving.

I stood there in awe watching the Seraph and looking around the yard at the children playing, and my husband saying his goodbyes to the family. Suddenly, in an instant, I was transported to 25 or so years into the future. I see that our goddaughter's son is now in his late 20's, standing near a motorcycle (his little bicycle had changed into a motorcycle), conversing with his father who had also aged appropriately 25 years. The little girl was missing. I realized she had transitioned (died) at some point in those 25 years. She was no longer in the body. The children's mother appeared to be no longer a part of this family. I had the feeling she was still in the body; I realized I could learn what she was doing and where she was, but I felt it to be ugly and I didn't want to see it—at least not in this moment. I was with the Seraph, and he had taken me into the future to show me something.

I didn't know what to make of this new information, and I didn't want to analyze it now. I wanted to experience the fullness of what I was being offered. I could trust that any meaning or messages would come at the appropriate time. I trust in Divine timing. I always have.

The limo came, and I gave my hugs and kisses and turned to leave. The tears were still flowing, and I was using every tissue in the box.

The Seraph appeared to me...

What did it all mean?

My husband tried to comfort me, as though I was sad because we were leaving these little ones. I told him the Seraph came to visit me. He is always supportive and encourages me through my spiritual awakenings. I felt as if I was still in the full experience of the Seraph when I placed my call to Ruth Rendely.

When I spoke with Ruth, she asked me about the size of the Seraph. I held the image so keenly in my mind, as I still do to this day. Hovering in the sky, he seemed transparent, yet I could clearly take in every detail of His features. It was helpful to compare His size to something relatable. My eyes scanned down to ground level as he floated above the garage in the sky, and he was larger than the condominium building where I live. I live in a seventeen-story high-rise. His enormous stature seemed to fill twenty-five percent of the sky. His presence inspired calm, trust, contentment and acceptance. His countenance neutral: all- knowing, balanced discernment. His energy seemed to extend to me and enfold me and offer me the experience of these qualities. Maybe this is an extension of the energy of Seraphim Grace which I had activated earlier. The vibration and continuance of this vibration is certainly grace and ease.

Why was I told to get down on my knees? I wondered. Ruth offered the idea that I was initially instructed to get down on my knees; otherwise, I would have fallen. She is probably right.

Why did the Seraph visit me? What was I supposed to do? What did it all mean? I had no idea.

That night, back home, as I went into my meditation, I began with prayers for our goddaughter and her family with the awareness that difficult situations were ahead for all of them. I had been shown that sweet little Caroline would be leaving this planet way too soon. In the state of meditation, I revisited my experience, allowing myself to drift back to that yard and the vision of the Seraph. As I did this, I now saw the Seraph and three angels hovering over the four corners of the property. The angels were much smaller than the Seraph. I wondered about the significance—three angels—forming a triangle?

As if my wondering were a question spoken out loud, I received the knowing answer that these are three angels now posted to assist the guardian angels of the four people who live in the home. The grid would remain in place, and the angels were to hold the space for their protection.

Protection.

I hadn't used the word protection in my thoughts or in my prayers for this family. But, truly, that was my heart's desire: protection for these sweet innocent child-beings amid human creation.

A few days later our goddaughter sent me this email:

> I am trembling as I write this note to you. I feel led to write to you as we so enjoyed having you stay with us while you were in town. Yesterday, we experienced a miracle in our home, and I feel as if your presence inspired it.
>
> The children were playing as my husband watched football in the TV room with friends from the neighborhood. I was getting the food together for the outside BBQ on this beautiful fall day.
>
> It could not have been more than 5 minutes, when I had this overwhelming feeling to check on the children. I knew my husband was in the same room with them, but it was almost like I was being pulled to check on them.

As I walked back down to the family room, friends were riveted to the TV, but my husband and children were not in the room. I looked out the sliding glass door and saw Ethan playing outside by the pool. Where was Caroline? I rushed out the door, and, to my horror, she was floating face down in the pool! I screamed and jumped in to pull her out. My husband helped to pull us out of the water; he had only been a few feet away trying to get the grill started when she must have fallen into the pool. She could catch her breath and cry—as we all cried together in panic, relief, and joy that our daughter, for the most part, was okay.

In an instant, everything could have changed. And everything has changed. The all-consuming fear that my husband and I felt when we realized we almost lost our most precious possession; the shame we feel at having failed to protect our child. Our children depend on us for all their needs, and how can we insure this never happens again? We are so grateful to have been given another chance to get it right.

My husband and I are struggling with our own internal blame. And though I have such gratitude that I "listened" and followed my intuition, we can't help but realize that it was a miracle. You hear the stories of parents and babysitters who say they simply "looked away for a few minutes", and then tragedy strikes; the baby drowns in the pool or lake, and the impact is felt for a lifetime. We experienced a miracle, and I want to feel the impact of that miracle for my lifetime.

I am writing to you, my sweet Maria, because I am asking for your prayers and energy healing support,

because I have decided to stop drinking and eliminate alcohol from my life. I will never forget the moment when we almost lost our precious Caroline. I cannot get the image out of my mind.... the moment I saw her lying in the pool. And now I want to focus on this second chance and become a better person, a better wife and mother. I can't help but wonder if this happened to allow me to truly appreciate all the blessings in my life?
Thank you.

This event occurred four days after the angels were posted.

Why did the Seraph show Himself to me? The answers are being revealed to me as I'm discovering more and more each day. Our goddaughter and her family have been redirected to a new timeline. Caroline's life was protected by the grid and the angels stationed at the corners of their property. The timeline that I was shown 25 years into the future has been changed. Angels can and do intervene for the good when we ask for their assistance.

Since this experience, I have been shown that I can post an angel with a child for protection. I can go back in time to a difficult situation or even to the time of their birth and post an angel for protection. The Seraph transmitted this to me. I do not need the Seraph to show himself to me to accomplish this. I am forever grateful to Divine Source Energy for the gifts I have been given, and I am honored to share the path of enlightenment through the Seraphim Blueprint.

Maria Sue Mutu Hubbuch, a retired Social Worker, born and raised in the Detroit suburbs, practices a life-long commitment to personal spiritual growth and being of service. In 2002, she met her husband Mark who introduced her to Kriya Yoga and Reiki, which began the journey of learning energy healing. Now a practitioner and teacher of Esoteric Healing®, ThetaHealing®, and Seraphim Blueprint®, she enjoys sharing these with others. Maria resides in Naples, Florida.

Fixing Creation

June 6, 2018

Yesterday, I was feeling especially discouraged with my life and the state of the world, and creation in general. I don't understand how creation could have so many problems and so much suffering; so, as I went to sleep last night, I felt like just giving up on trying to fix it.

When I awoke this morning, I decided to meditate first, rather than doing my usual routine, and then meditate. The advantage for me in doing this is that there's nothing in my system like caffeine or food to keep me up on the surface. As I started to meditate, I remembered how frustrated I was with the Earth and creation, and how slowly the ascension process seemed to be going where everyone is focused on fixing what is now, bit by bit. Then I had the thought to change creation at its very first moment, even before it began, and then everything that unfolded after that would be better.

The reason I had this thought goes back to a healing session I had with a Theta healer here in Minnesota. In one of those sessions, we went back to the beginning of my time in this creation, and we were told that the Creator first began creating souls in small batches, like cookies, and the first batch was thirteen souls, and I was the oldest of them. We were told that my name at that time was Jehovah, and the youngest of the batch was a girl named Crystal Oracle. Now, I don't know if my name then has anything at all to do with modern day religions. Many people have the same names, so I doubt there's a connection.

Anyway, after we were created, we weren't given any instructions in what to do except "not to look behind a veil" which covered up all the possible different creation time lines that the Creator could choose from. Well, that was too much of a temptation for Crystal Oracle, so she looked behind the veil. She saw the almost infinite array of possible choices of different creations, but her attention locked onto a most terrifying one. Then she came running out and told us all about it. We became so concerned that we decided that we needed to fix that one, which, unbeknownst to us, caused that one to be the one that was selected to play out.

We don't know why the Creator allowed that to happen, or why he didn't change it or set it right, but, apparently, at that time, the Creator was more indifferent and wanted to experience all possibilities and didn't realize how it would affect the beings in his creation. This caused me to be very angry with the Creator. How could he put us in that situation, new souls with no instructions or guidance other than "don't look behind the veil", and then, when one among us did, why he didn't help us, or guide us out of that situation? So, you might say, I've held a grudge for a long time. I've tried repeatedly to forget it, to forgive the Creator, to accept responsibility and stop blaming him, etc., etc., but nothing really worked other than just not thinking about it.

However, this morning, rather than being angry or regretting the mistake, I decided to just change it. In recent years, Divine Mother has given me many divine energies to work with, and two of them have to do with undoing past events. The names are simple, but the effects are powerful. The first is called "Undo", and it can be applied to situations and events that I want to undo and change. The second is called "Oops" (Divine Mother has a sense of humor), and it is used whenever I do something with all good intention, but for unforeseen reasons, it turns out poorly, and I want to undo it. The energies are very similar, but, apparently, slightly different.

So, I decided to change that first mistake of this creation, and I began running "Undo" on Crystal Oracle and her choice to look behind the veil, and I ran "Undo" and "Oops" for almost an hour to make sure that this mistake never occurred. When I finished, the timeline was changed, and Crystal Oracle never looked behind the veil, and I replaced her mistake with an understanding that we would accept whichever timeline the Creator chose. This alone took a huge burden off me, and I felt significantly lighter and happier. The original mistake was changed, I didn't have to be angry at the Creator, and the entire timeline of creation could now change for the better.

Then, I began moving from that original beginning point on the timeline forward while sending "Undo" and "Oops" to this original thick dark timeline all the way to the present. I then went back to make sure the original mistake was still erased, and I ran a little more "Undo" just to be sure. Next, I went to work on the timeline again, but this time, the entire timeline was encased in something that looked like a caterpillar's cocoon, and I got the strong impression that it was now in the process of being changed and that I shouldn't mess with it anymore while it was going through this transformation or metamorphosis. That was unexpected, but also very cool and inspiring to see.

But, true to my nature, I thought that if I can undo that first mistake and change the entire timeline of creation to something that I hoped and expected would be much better, depending on what the Creator chose, then why can't I add these divine energies that Divine Mother has given me to that beginning point and thereby make creation even better, or at least more to our liking? So, I went back to the beginning and started running divine energies like "Lively Unbounded Divine Love" and "Love is the Answer". Then I ran "The Golden Rain of Divine Wealth and Prosperity" but stopped that one because I wasn't sure I wanted this creation to be focused even more on wealth and prosperity. Then I added a little more "Lively Unbounded Love", but decided to stop there because now I was no longer allowing the Creator to choose how He wanted this creation; I was choosing the way I wanted it to be.

So, this raises many interesting questions worthy of a sci-fi movie, or a philosophy class. The first is, was this real or just my imagination; and if it was real, will it affect just me or all of creation, and how will there be change and how quickly? Other questions might be: If this is real, did I have the right to do it? Will most people be happier because of it? What does the Creator think about it? Will we notice changes as the metamorphosis happens, or will there just be change, and we won't even notice it since we won't remember the old and bad way because that never would have occurred? Pretty deep, eh?

So, I called my friend David, who's in Unity Consciousness and has been my guide and coach on much of this journey, and left a voice message for him describing the experience. He then called back a couple of hours later, after checking with Divine Mother and others, and said that what I did was perfect, 100% good, and that now I should wait about three weeks or so for the changes to take place and then decide if I want to add more divine energies or just "Let the Creator have a jolly good time with it". I also have to decide over the next few weeks whether I want to remember how things were before so that I can marvel at what a huge change has taken place and how wonderful it is; or do I just want the changes to take place smoothly and innocently without remembering how bad it was before? The benefit of not remembering the old is that everything is pure and innocent, untarnished by the painful memories of the old creation. No one would know it was ever anything different. The advantage of remembering is to be happy and thrilled at how much of a change was brought about, but there's also the possibility of dwelling on the memories and re-introducing sadness, anger, grief etc. into the new creation. Also, there's the question of "who" will remember the difference, just me or everyone? That may make a huge difference in my decision because, if it's just me, then the risk of tarnishing the new present is less, but if everyone can remember, there may be much more opportunity to backslide.

However, here we go back into sci-fi land. What would it be like to be the only person in creation to remember what it was like before? Could you, or should you, ever tell anyone at all; would they believe you, or would they lock you up and feed you dumb-dumb pills to make you normal? Would it drive you crazy or make you very gratified? Or is this just my imagination and I should write sci-fi movie scripts? The problem is we may never know whether it's real or not if I choose to have none of us remember the old and bad timeline. In that case, the mistake was never made, and I never had to have this experience, and no changes to the timeline were done.

John Chandler began studying Seraphim Blueprint Energies in 2007 and has been an enthusiastic teacher since 2010. He has been a certified teacher of Transcendental Meditation since 1971 and has been working with Divine Mother, the Seraph, and other Divine Beings to bring out new Divine Energies over the past seven years. He teaches courses online and by teleconference. He resides in Chanhassen, Minnesota on the west side of Minneapolis.

The Dolphin

Settling Down

As we slowly left the dock at our friend's house in Palm Isles, excitement and expectancy was permeating us all. We were having a day to escape the quarantine effects of Covid19. My daughter, Jennifer, and her two sons had flown down, leaving the strict lockdowns prevalent in North Carolina. Visiting me in Florida where we have some movement, albeit cautious, brought a welcome, happy sanctuary to a mother with two young, continually active boys. The radiating sun was shining brightly, giving us its welcomed warmth on this late spring day. Gorgeous cirrus and cumulus clouds, in perfect white layers and puffs, floated peacefully in the sky with an intense vivid blue background offering artistic images for an active imagination to gaze upon.

It only took us ten minutes at idle speed, protecting the fragile mangrove banks and momma manatees, to get into Hurricane Bay. It was time to turn up the speed, throttle down. We felt like we were flying as the crisp salty spray glanced off our cheeks, wetting our lips and flinging our hair to and fro. We held on tight to the little ones who were now no longer trying to remove their cumbersome life jackets. A big smile was on everyone's face. The almost four-year-old

JJ was sitting in Katy's lap, my son's boat savvy co-captain and wonderful wife. In this high seat, he could watch the instruments mapping our way to Sanibel Island and see the sonar ping off the bottom, sharing its wisdom of how deep the water is and where the fish are.

The tiny islands we whizzed by were filled with nesting egrets, seagulls, anhingas, osprey, pelicans, and a variety of herons. The fish were jumping as well, accompanied by the occasional dolphin rolling its familiar fin and gracefully breaking the water's surface. It was quiet time as my mechanically-minded son John's 27' fishing boat with twin outboard engines sped effortlessly across the silky-smooth waters. I could feel all the parts of my brain relaxing and influencing the healing powers of the vagus nerve. My parasympathetic nervous system was having a massage, much like the work of a Cranial Sacral treatment. This settling peace and comfort was tingling through all my visceral organs, endocrine system, my bones, and my blood down to the tips of my toes. I could sense the movement of the magnetic energy from the Seraphim Blueprint attunements effortlessly activated. It felt like I was flying with the screeching birds, rolling with the dancing dolphins, journeying into the scene the clouds offered in the play before me.

I do not know how long it was before we rounded the corner of Matanzas Pass. Ten minutes, ten hours, time had stood still because I was engrossed in the presence of now. Magic had happened. We gently idled westward between San Carlos Beach and Fort Myers Beach. The myriad creatures of the beach and of the boating businesses filled the banks of the pass. Every few minutes, a sunken boat, and even shrimp trawlers, jetted partially out of the water, having met their functional end during one of the many hurricanes at the aptly named Hurricane Bay. As the occupants of our fishing boat were oohing and aahing, I could not help but wonder what the lives of the inhabitants and visitors along the banks, present and past, were like. So many people represented, from the ultra-wealthy yacht owner to the simple, yet proud, friendly fisherman, and all walks of life between. How large is our world? Do we really know people and who they are, where they come from, their joys, their struggles? What if…

"May I have a drink?" Jefferson asks.

Jarred back to now, I reached into the worn red cooler to get my two-year-old thirsty grandson a juice box. We settled back to our safe positions as we rounded the northern tip of Bowditch Point Park to prepare to zoom across a bit of the Gulf of Mexico towards Sanibel Island. This well-known and popular shelling spot offers 250 types of shells due to its east-west positioning as a prime sift from the Gulf. We went about a quarter of the way along the 15-mile narrow island to find a perfect spot to anchor, one sandy and calm enough to walk to shore and, more importantly, without people.

Wading to shore with kids, a cooler of watermelon, sandwiches and Shandy and with dry bags over our shoulders, we saw a slithering school of eleven sting rays in a diamond formation, cascading along the rippled shore. No worries! We settled in amongst the hundreds of sandpipers and seagulls while the young ones were gleefully running into these flocks of birds causing them to rise and quickly resettle just out of reach of the laughing boys. As this play continued, clearly the unaffected yet attentive birds had experienced human children before and maintained the play for a chance at stealing a morsel of something to eat.

We were so content. My daughter and I walked a few steps north together. Having completed all the Seraphim Blueprint levels, Jenny touched her elevated spirit in a sensitive and intentioned way. As masters of our world, we both treasure the ability to merge with the beings on our Earth for wisdom, insight, and delight. Protection and healing continuously flow within us. The beauty of the environment and the heartbeat of nature rise into our souls as she and I looked up to the exquisite, streaming formations of cirrus clouds.

Jenny instantly gasped, "John Alan is here!" I concurred. We both intimately felt the presence of Jenny's first child, one with us for 8 months and 29 days, whose human heartbeat stopped three days before his expected birth. He was here with his brothers, chasing the seagulls. Clear as an angel in the clouds, our hearts raced in knowing we just don't really know all there is to know. We took a picture of John Alan, this grand cirrus cloud, a memory captured and a presence easily connected to when missing him. This wasn't the first time Jenny experienced John Alan. He has made his presence known to her, to Jamey, to her sons, to me, to many. She shared this sweet observation with her husband Jamey who was working very hard at an essential job back home. Being the attuned dad that he is he texted back, "I wondered. I just felt him also. That's cool."

Reflection

We didn't think about the 18 months of life between the last heartbeat of John Alan and the birth of Jamey Jr. The mother's emotional pain that comes with birthing a passed-on child is inconceivable unless borne. The father's fragile untouchable heartbreak for not holding his long-awaited son combined with fruitlessly holding an inconsolable spouse, is without comparison to the depth of the tragedy. There is no 'getting over' this loss, however often well-meaning, yet woefully unaware friends advise you to. While one doesn't ever get over such loss, there is nevertheless growth of wisdom. Why would you want to get over such an experience? Only in diving into the essence of the message can wholeness come. There is revealed the recognition of our power to create a world to live in that can accept and even forgive the death of a life not given the chance to live. One may even ponder what is living? Can one live without a body? Is there growth of a soul without the experience of a human body?

What of the global deaths due to COVID19, the lockdowns, the loss of relationship and opportunity to socialize? What of the economic and business losses, the destruction of community and future financial security? Did one extraordinary loss of life prepare one to know how to experience a pandemic? Is this COVID19 pandemic a cover up of an even more sinister child trafficking horror being conquered, revealed, and alleviated? Is the pandemic simply a human reaction to the manipulation of electricity and microwaves permeating the skies and heavens through the implementation of a 5G global communication network? Do we really have any power to help ourselves? How do we create a safe world with personal power in which to live happily with care, compassion, concern and comradery?

There are great thinkers who study esoteric and exoteric thought. Others study the quantum physics of the brain from the perspective of science or even of PSI. We research intuition, precognition, clairvoyance, remote viewing and so very much more. Can we talk to animals, to crystals, to God? Can we hear them talk back without being considered schizophrenic? That which communicates beyond our five senses, using all the magnetism and matter of existence, can give us the power to influence our own experience and perhaps even create our own experience. How much does our experience of beauty affect others? In this time of COVID19, how strong are we to not be negatively influenced by the experience of separation or violence? How capable are we to meditate with intention and apply our positive experience with angels, Jesus, or other loving energies that heal humanity with healthy, high vibrations and valuable thought?

The stillness which moves, and the silence which speaks that comes with meditation, teaches us of our power, of our mind. With skill and dedication, practice and perfection, we learn. The call of those departed encourages us to seek even more. The worlds of other great masters of thought invoke us to listen, and in that to hear their wisdom as well as their warning. We learn how to have the effects of a glorious boat ride even if inside. We learn to look at the clouds and hear from beyond, or is it from within? Mother Mary presents herself in many ways. Others of holy mastership reveal their worlds to us. Can we hear them? We can and we must envision our world with safety and beauty and gratefulness.

We are grateful to Ruth Rendely who channeled the Seraph in 1994, bringing us the Seraphim Blueprint system of healing and personal growth. Who knew we would learn about DNA manipulation and the need to return our DNA to its original state? Or that we would need light to cleanse our cells, or need to reconnect our soul with our Creator?

That we can experience living through another's perspective allows a connection of understanding, invoking forgiveness and compassion. That we can call in the rising of our Kundalini in a gentle controlled way to absorb the fullness of our own infinite mystery is a treasure beyond measure. Having the ability to protect ourselves from the ill effects of 5G waves, radiation, or perhaps required vaccines, or weakened food gives us comfort. We turn away from fear, the "False Evidence Appearing Real" and towards Love, Light and Consciousness. Feeling connected to the source in silence and timelessness leaves one in such peace that description is impossible.

Nature can come alive and bring her colors and waves of magic to minister to the hurting and needy. Nature within our Creator brings us her dance. As the sun rises and the sun sets, the whisper of the tween times woos us to believe in ourselves, to stop and smell the roses, letting the lingering sweet scent of her beauty show us our glory, all the while protecting us with a thorny armor from the encroaching storm.

Rising

No, as we gazed upon those angelic cirrus clouds, we didn't reflect on life from John Alan's last heartbeat to now. That was already in us. In this moment, we were timeless. The alchemy of all thought brought us to this moment of glory, promising more to come. Turning our gaze from the clouds showering the light of John Alan, we returned to the group and opened the cooler filled with fresh-cut watermelon. Excited cries of 'I want some' exploded from the bouncing boys doing their happy dance. There is little as satisfying as being on the beach and allowing the satiating sweet pink juice of this marvelous fruit glide down the cheeks, down the chest and onto the sand making those cute pink droplets of art. From minutes to long moments to making marvelous memories, the experiences kept on coming. Live coquinas wiggled through our toes if we stood long enough to allow the waves to rush upon the shore and recede as quickly. Tiny minnows took nips of our legs, creating a sustained giggle. Cockle shells, corals, mermaids' tails, turkey wings, cones and crowns, clams, murexes, drills and millions of shells (I'm not exaggerating) were scattered on the beach, several broken in the process of being pulverized into fine sand, others amazingly whole, waiting for a trip to our mantle, or glass keepsake jar.

The aqua green water was quite clear, and, in the shallow water, we could see to the bottom. By now, we had seen several schools of sting rays and repeated delights of dolphins rolling in both groups and singly. I had walked out to the sandbar, which had me standing in waist-deep water near our boat. I had seen dolphins playing and felt an urge to get closer. Because I had walked away from the contented group on the shore, the sounds of the happy talk faded away. I called in the energy of speaking to the animals from my Seraphim Blueprint attunements. I began to hear sonic-type sounds. Were they coming from the dolphin or from the sounds of the spheres in the galaxy?

There was a single dolphin then diving ten meters south of the boat. I was at the edge of the sand bar near the open water. My heart was both racing and calm. I felt fully alive and attuned in a very open hypersensitive way. I was now about three meters from this dolphin, watching him closely. He swam to the left, and five meters away, he turned and swam to the right, again turning back at five meters away. He went back and forth, getting as close as two meters when he was in front of me. He was on his side and always showing a bit of his white belly as he propelled himself past me. Occasionally, he was so slow, it was as if he was not even trying to move. His upward eye was looking at me. I didn't know whether to breathe or not. I talked to him with my mind. Saying hello, I thanked him for sharing his water with me. I told him I like him and am as curious about him as I believe he is about me. He told me he knows me. He said he has swum with me before. I thought to myself that I should be surprised at that, but, deeper inside, I know it is true. However, this was the first time I had gotten this close. We deepened our conversation. He told me I have grown. He said that more animals are communicating with me now. He told me I heard a lot more about everything than I used to. He told me I am well prepared for this life of healing and the coming years. He told me he has seen me in other dimensions too. He showed me much to confirm my interdimensional travel. It was not in a language expressible in words. I was feeling amazed, yet out of sorts to be having such a profound experience in the setting of nature with so many people around. People! My family!

I turned back towards shore and waved to my son who had begun to walk towards me with JJ on his shoulders. He had noticed me being so close to this dolphin. They came as close as eight meters behind me and were now on the sandbar. Sitting on John's shoulders, JJ could see the dolphin gliding back and forth in front of me. The dolphin told me he knows JJ too and that he can see the angels. He told me John Alan is well and doing important work for many beings, human and others. He told me John Alan talks to JJ, and JJ hears him and knows that it is his brother in heaven. A part of me drifted in and said I am making this up, but, instantly, that doubting thought popped like a soap bubble and floated with its iridescent colors into the ethers, leaving me filled with a significant knowingness. This was as real as the hologram of me. I thanked the dolphin for his sharing. We touched hearts. He told me he has been with me in many forms over much time. I asked him if he was an angel? He replied, "Aren't we all?" And then he winked. I saw that wink. I did, I did! I realized the light had caught his rarely blinking eyelid in such a way as to reflect a wink. I felt him realize that I noticed how he did that. Undoubtedly smiling, he swam away.

"We are all angels?" I asked myself, radiating in the question. My son and JJ waited for me as we sauntered back to shore. I was stunned silent in a perfected knowingness of peace. Jumping down from John's shoulders, JJ ran up to his mom and said, "I talked to the dolphin. Did you see me?"

"Yes dear, I saw you," Jenny replied kindly.

"Can we do it again?" JJ asked.

"One day yes, another day," Jenny added, knowing there would indeed be another day.

An experience like that splits your mind. A part of you relives the experience as you replay your thoughts and feelings. Another part of you listens to family, engaging in the touch and laughter of intrigue and joy, simple stories, and total satisfaction.

The sandwiches had been eaten and the watermelon was all gone. Packing up, we ventured through the waters back to the boat. We had gotten a bit of sun, which showed its glow on our skin, since, by now, the sunscreen had worn off. Repositioning ourselves, with towels covering the little ones, we were ready for a brief nap while heading home. The waves had heightened because offshore winds were blowing, and a bit of bumpiness accompanied our sensory overload. The color of the water was strikingly beautiful. Had it ever been this green, or was it Caribbean blue, or was it an aqua color? I thought it was truly the deepest green I had ever seen. I took pictures and looked at the phone; alas, it could not capture the intensity of these green waters. As I was thinking about this color on the water, Jenny shouted across the wind to me, "Do you see how green the water is?" I nodded emphatically, happy that more people than I had noticed. I was having a shared experience.

We arrived once again at the pass that runs between Fort Myers and San Carlos beach. We idled past the homes, condos, boat houses, bars and businesses, but now feeling the connectedness of all that is. Curiosity and questions had subsided. Peace on earth I have. There was beauty everywhere, even in the sunken boats and the dilapidated shrimp trawlers. Beingness was at its full capacity. It was well with my soul. I understood that everyone's world adds to mine as mine adds to theirs. Further, the more I see beauty, the more beauty there is. Let us remember beauty and be thankful. Let us own our feelings, our world, our universe. Let us not be influenced by fear. Let us be of the great I Am which is Love. My experience with the beach, my family, John Alan, and the dolphin has made my world better, and in that your world is better also. For the world, may we continue to make our worlds better places to live, to love, to dance, to laugh and to create.

Lucy Finch has been a student and teacher of Seraphim Blueprint for eight years. The awareness of this systems' unique personal empowering potential has replaced her skilled use of Reiki, TM, Theta, Esoteric, EFT, Reconnective Healing and more. As an owner of a metaphysical/crystal store called Altered Elements in Naples, Florida, she continues to use sound and crystal healing combined with Seraphim Blueprint.

Becoming Enlightened

To Search is Divine...

For as long as we have gazed at the stars, we've wondered at the vastness of the universe and questioned our nature. Where did we come from, and where are we headed?

For some, asking those questions implies the existence of a higher power, such as God, or All That Is. For others, such questions are moot because they don't believe there is a God.

But if you do choose to believe in a Divine Being and want answers to your questions about life, and the universe, where do you look? There are so many paths, so many authoritative-sounding voices claiming to know the path to God.

They can't all be entirely true, can they? But they can't all be totally wrong, either. Isn't it said there's a thread of truth running through them all?

Undoubtedly, the nature of God is the great mystery of the ages. Just asking the right questions can be a challenge, not to mention finding answers that make sense when you put them all together.

But no matter how you may search, simply searching is essential. The searching is your path to answers. Searching for God is the way to enlightenment. Enlightenment and secrets about angels.

If it were you who had found answers, had found enlightenment, you'd want to tell people about it, wouldn't you? Or would you keep it hidden, hiding your light under a bushel?

I ask because I'm that guy who found enlightenment. I've been enlightened for over 30 years, and I've largely kept it hidden.

I'll tell you a bit about how I became enlightened and my thoughts on angels I encountered on the path. There are a few open secrets about angels, too. Hold on to your comfort blanket; you could find this to be a bumpy ride.

Angels Have the Wow Factor

Angels have different meanings to different people. Everyone who experiences angels sees them in a unique way through the lens of their own beliefs and perceptions.

Some people believe in the concept of evil, or mischievous angels of some kind. Most people view angels as emissaries of God.

My perception is that angels are forces for good. Whatever angels tell you was thought up by God. Angels are like God in a form that we can easily understand. They're not as blindingly intense as being in the direct presence of God, like a filter that lets you look directly at the splendour of a solar eclipse. Angels are God Lite.

You could also say of angels that when you meet one, there's no doubt about what you're seeing. It's an angel, and you immediately go, "Wow!" An angel encounter will affect you for days and years afterwards.

And there are commonalities in the experiences of most people who have encountered positive angels. Something usual about angels, for example, is they seem to turn up at just the right moment. It's as if they knew what was going to happen before it happened, and they appear at precisely the right time. Our perception of time is linear, but angels experience time differently and can see what's happening along our time line and step in, so to speak. They're undoubtedly masters of timing.

They usually bring a message, too. You don't get an angel appearing just so they can socialize or chat to you about the weather or chastise you because you forgot to do the dishes. We can say that angels are highly intentional. And the message they bring is usually easy to understand and to agree with. It's often profound and usually uplifting, like "Peace on Earth." Angels would never drop by your place to trash-talk your ex, for example. Angels have class.

Enlightened but Not an Angel

As an enlightened person, I've got a way to go before I pass out of this physical world and evolve into an angel. Just give me time—we all grow up eventually. For now, though, I'm just an ordinary dude who got enlightened early in life and has spent decades getting comfortable with it here in our physical world.

If you're an angel, on the other hand, you're living in a different place than this physical world. And although, as an angel, you don't live on Earth with its wars and disasters and taxes, you can reach across to this physical place to offer messages of wisdom and hope. Then you go back to your spiritual home in a higher place without being embedded in this world, so to speak. Commuting is part of your job description.

Getting to the place where you become an angel yourself,

that's much further down the track. That's for when we've left this physical realm behind and have moved on to the happiness and beauty of non-physical reality. Some people call that place 'heaven'.

I, on the other hand, do live here. And along with all the blessings in my life, I also have to deal with the banal. I need to delete spam emails and pay my taxes and live with the new reality of the COVID19 pandemic, for example. To paraphrase Buddha, "Before enlightenment: cook meals, wash dishes. After enlightenment: cook meals, wash dishes."

Do Enlightened People Make Mistakes?

And here's an associated question I've often asked myself: Which is more challenging, the effort it takes to become enlightened, or living as an enlightened person in an unenlightened world? Anyway, everyone who becomes enlightened—as we all eventually do—experiences enlightenment through their own perceptions.

So, I'm bound by the physical world and its realities, both good and bad, to put it in black and white terms. Often, though, it's the grey areas that can present the real challenges. In some respects, it's taken me years to learn to discern where I end and where other people begin, for example. That may sound absurd, but when you're enlightened, you see everything as a whole. It's fundamental to know that we each have our own everlasting sense of self, while, at the same time, we're also part of everything.

So, in terms of spiritual maturity and living as a physical person, consider that much of what we do is influenced by the thoughts and actions of those around us. You can't make the right choices all the time; you just have to make the best choices you can. In other words, I'm enlightened, but just like everyone else, I've made mistakes and I'll continue to make mistakes. Mostly though, I seem to make fewer these days.

Angels Leave You Wanting More

Angels, on the other hand, have an unblemished record. They never seem to make mistakes. Everything they do is guided by goodness.

When an angel appears before you, it has moral authority. It ranks more highly than you. Angels have gravitas and power. That's what angels do and what they are.

Angels are fleeting, too. They're not physical beings like us. They usually appear for only a short while. Sometimes they look like beautiful, glowing humans with wings; sometimes they take other forms. They often don't appear to be solid. They're there one minute, and then they're gone all too quickly, leaving you wanting more.

Not everybody can see angels, but consider also that angels don't appear to just anybody. Certainly, an angel won't appear to someone who's not ready to see one. Your thoughts need to be elevated before you can be receptive to an angel.

There May Be Angels in Your Future

I've had four angel encounters. Your own angel encounter may not be easy to share with others, and it's not always something that you should.

It's interesting to me that two of my most profound angel encounters have yet to take place, but I can see them and feel them clearly well advanced in my future. I can thank my enlightenment for the psychic ability to see fleeting phenomena like that, occurrences that are most likely to happen, but that have not yet happened.

Enlightenment Is Highly Recommended

So, let's shift gears from angels to enlightenment and higher spiritual attainment—which can be achieved in the here and now in this physical world. Since I'm enlightened, I feel compelled to encourage you to pursue your higher purpose, so here are my thoughts on enlightenment and how I achieved it. Of course, you'll always find your own path in a way that's uniquely yours, but I can at least give you a few general directions.

I've often wondered why isn't everyone trying to become enlightened? It's worth all the effort because, once you get here, it's awesome. One advantage of being enlightened is that you automatically gain a certain degree of psychic ability, and who wouldn't want that?

The answer is that most people aren't actively searching for enlightenment or even considering it. They go about their daily lives and give little thought to looking deep within themselves to discover their Godhood. And, although you may not see it from where you currently stand, you'll eventually get there, like a caterpillar in a cocoon slowly becomes something different through a miraculous transformation.

Early on in life, I spent a lot of time deeply considering and questioning the state of my own being. I had a compelling thought that it was possible to find answers to life, the universe and everything, and I wasn't going to compromise or stop until I'd found it because I concluded that this was the highest attainment of mankind. It felt like I was on the edge of it. There was to be no turning back. I just knew it was out there for me to find if I looked with an open heart.

I considered myself to be a true seeker. I would have contently lived my entire life always seeking a spiritual path, always looking to find the hidden meanings, always striving for enlightenment. As it turns out, I didn't have to strive for too long. I was so persistent and demanding of answers that I soon found them.

Self-Realization at 17

At the age of 17, I had a breakthrough. It was as if the universe was telling me that I was on the right path, that loving spiritual energy was guiding me, that I just needed to keep asking questions. Psychic experiences can be difficult to describe with words, but it felt as though I suddenly had a greater awareness of reality and of my own thinking.

My subconscious became more acutely conscious, and that was a big deal because it was the key to becoming a master of my own thoughts. It happened in an instant, a moment of deep insight, and with it, I now had a different kind of inner vision that I had never been aware of before.

It was as though I was given an additional sense because, now, I could see everything vibrating with a kind of inner light, a spiritual light. I see that there's light everywhere. That early era of my life was the self-realization phase, a warm- up for full-on enlightenment.

What Is Enlightenment, Anyway?

When I talk about enlightenment, I'm talking about a sudden and full-on massive psychic experience that connects you with the universe in an unequivocally real and profound way. When I attained enlightenment, it was overwhelming, and now, even more than thirty years later, I still find it over-whelming occasionally.

When I became enlightened, I instantly became a different person, though still myself. My mind was so wonderfully transformed, it took me several years to fully find my way back to me. With enlightenment, I entered a secret world, but a world in plain sight.

Enlightenment Is All That and More

Enlightenment came quickly. It was all over in a series of moments. It seems like one minute I was asking myself a bunch of questions about spiritual matters, and the next moment a series of doors opened, as though I had an insight or an answer that opened one door, and that opened the next door and the next.

I realize these were symbols I created to make it easier for me to understand what was going on. When the final door opened, it was as though I was looking straight into God. I felt utterly fulfilled. There was a sudden sense that, yeah, I totally get it now. This is what God is, and I'm part of it. I'd finally found what I'd been yearning for. It felt like being reunited with a loved one. It felt like home. It felt timeless, eternal.

You Are We

A moment later, it felt like a loving hand gently reached into my awareness and opened a vast multitude of channels of consciousness for me to observe. It was like the universe of thought was being introduced and curated for me, showing me how to tune in to different channels. In one instance, for example, it was as though I felt different forms of mass consciousness, all with different characteristics, all a part of me, and me a part of them.

A 20-Year Old with a Secret

It was a lot for me to handle. It was as though my mind was forming from birth, but, this time, with super consciousness built in, and all my previous memories were unaffected. For months afterwards, I was so inside my own head that I became quiet and had difficulty forming even basic sentences in conversation, partly because I felt part of everyone.

Everything seemed so profound then, so I chose my words with much more precision. It seemed, too, that, as I spoke, the words were just symbols for a deeper communication. It took about a decade or so for me to finally get back to being socially adept.

Comfortably 30

At this point, I was getting much better at small talk and all kinds of talk, for that matter. I realized that I had to be adept at communicating in all situations. I was also still learning to be comfortable in my own skin.

I continued to flex and explore my psychic muscles, and they continued to develop. I also enjoyed months-long solo stints deep in the wilderness, fasting, meditating and observing the genius of nature.

Finding a Way at 40

Life became easier the more adept I became, and I began to use my enlightenment as a tool. I got much better at what I like to call artful living. That's the ability to create positive situations for yourself and others.

My consciousness had become more discerning, prudent, worldlier, and wiser. While enjoying being this comfortable with my spiritual gifts, I wasn't yet ready to be a guru.

The View from 50

By now, I was a gifted communicator, continuing to discover how to live with my enlightenment. I easily shift into and out of trances and tune into gestalts of consciousness as second nature. Naturally, I'll have much more to say about enlightenment in other writings. It really is thrilling beyond words.

A Guru or Something Like That

As an enlightened person, I know that a goal in my life is to guide others on the path to enlightenment. I can do this subtly, such as through the example of how I live my life every day around loved ones and colleagues. I can do it more directly, such as through this writing. I have an amazing gift, and I want nothing more than to pay it forward. No matter what I do, I'll keep trying to do that in one way or another.

If you didn't know I was enlightened when you met me, would you recognize it? No. There's no light shining out of my head or anything like that (smile). If, on the other hand, someone told you that I was enlightened, and you asked me if I would give you spiritual guidance, I would.

If you remained open to my teachings, ours would become a lifelong relationship, and love and trust would be built as you found yourself moving closer to enlightenment. In other words, if the situation were right, I would dedicate part of my life to your spiritual growth. That's what gurus do. They have students.

Enlightenment and Credibility Go Hand in Hand

It's a pretty bold claim to say, "I'm enlightened." It's natural and normal for people to want to scrutinize that claim, hold it up to a standard that they have in their mind for what's real and what's not. Of course, that's if they even believe in the concept of enlightenment in the first place.

Since I'm defining enlightenment as an attainment independent of religion, many will cling to the comfort blanket of religious or other doctrine and reject the notion that someone could attain enlightenment outside of their belief system. If you can get past that, what does an enlightened person look like?

In the new age fashion, perhaps our ideal enlightened sadhu has brown skin and a long white beard and wears robes and lives in a cave in the Himalayas. And what kinds of miracles can he perform? Everybody knows that an enlightened person can move objects with their mind, right? Or can they?

Make no mistake, I'm the real deal. As such, my credibility is key. Remaining anonymous is the best way for me to maintain that credibility at this early stage of my coming out. I have many interesting and unique points to say about this, including why I choose to reveal my enlightenment only in certain ways and in certain circumstances. I'm saving that for another time.

There Is No Secret Society

I hasten to add that I've never much liked the concept of secret societies when it comes to spiritual matters. Perhaps I've resented the notion that there is a form of spiritual knowledge that's obtainable only to select social or ethnic or gender groups.

Rather, spiritual knowledge is neither exclusive nor privileged, but is always freely and openly available for those who seek it with honesty and altruism and without reservation.

Angels and Spiritual Guides Light the Path

Someone once said that if you seek God, seek God everywhere—also, that God is in the unexpected. For some, that seeking includes angels who often appear as messengers of God, or representatives of something deep and joyfully spiritual and profound. And just as angels can point us to a path of love and harmony, so, too, can a spiritual guide who has attained enlightenment.

There are many paths up the mountain, but at certain places they follow the same established course. Knowing where to find these paths is a key to opening your mind to the beautiful world that includes the dream state and what's beyond our physical form.

It's taken me three decades to be comfortable enough about my gift of enlightenment to want to talk about it and share it with you. I'm doing that in stages, and writing this is a start. And I'm available if you're seeking a spiritual guide—kindly contact me through the editor of this book.

Anonymous. The author is a creative polymath who has lived and worked in several countries during a career spanning the arts, media, industry, healthcare, government, charities and more. The author is also a founding member of an open discussion group that has persisted for over two decades, meeting regularly to discuss and explore spirituality and philosophy.

The Seraph Opens Israel

From the beginning, I knew there was something compelling about the process. About two years ago, my cousin Robert called to say that he received a letter from the Ministry of Justice of Israel. It had been forwarded to him from a previous address, and its contents were puzzling, suggesting that we might inherit property in Israel. He felt it was possibly a scam. He emailed me a copy of the letter, and, when I read it, I noticed it was written on normal governmental letterhead with a telephone number and a physical address in Jerusalem. I suggested to him that I call that number to see what I could find out. My cousin was willing to hand over the matter to me, even though my sister and his brother were also involved. I soon discovered that, of the four of us, I was the only one interested in exploring this matter.

The letter inquired whether we were the descendants of our grandfather, and mentioned that he had property in Israel that we might inherit. Now, governments don't usually give descendants decades to decide such matters, so the whole scenario was highly strange. Our grandfather died in 1970, and now it was 2018, forty-eight years later. So, when I called the number, my first question was why they were just contacting us after all this time. The polite man who answered the phone said, "Because before the existence of the internet, it was difficult to find anyone." Then I asked why wouldn't the government simply confiscate the land? And he answered, "Because Israel is not like other governments."

So, I started to think this was real and that my grandfather had either forgotten about his "property", which could either be land or other valuables, or he was keeping it a secret from the family because none of us knew anything about this. Since our parents were deceased, there were no remaining family members to ask. After doing research about land purchases in Israel in the 1920s, I assumed that my grandfather, an orthodox Jew, probably purchased land there to support a two-thousand-year-old Jewish collective desire to have a homeland again. I remembered from my childhood hearing him read prayers on high holidays ending with the repetitive phrase imploring God to let us celebrate the holidays "next year in Jerusalem".

Then, once I recognized that the information was likely legitimate, the Israeli Ministry of Justice wanted written proof, such as wills, birth and death certificates, and signatures to authenticate that we were the true descendants of Avraham Popil. Thus began a protracted process.

Most of our family's births and deaths occurred in New York State, and simply ordering birth and death certificates to be sent to Israel was insufficient for international verification. The Israeli government wanted "apostilles" for each certificate, which is an internationally recognized form of notarization, and the process of acquiring such involved several different state governmental agencies, each taking a fee for their services. After several months of negotiating these requirements, I was also required to check in with either an

Israeli consulate, or the Israeli Embassy in Washington. Since we live about two hours from the Atlanta Israeli Consulate, my husband and I went there to have them notarize all our documents. This took several hours, while the Consulate General copied them and then affixed a special red seal to each, which I could then forward on to Israel.

At that point, I still didn't know what sort of property my grandfather had owned. When the appropriate person at the Ministry of Justice saw my application, however, he told me that my grandfather had purchased 900 square meters of land (about a quarter-acre block) in northern Israel, zoned agricultural. He would not give me the address or exact location, however, because the internal committee within the Ministry of Justice hadn't yet decided our case. Discovering this would take another five months.

So, when in September of 2019, I still had not heard from this special committee about where my application stood, I contacted Mr. Aharon Shindler, the lawyer in charge, to ask what was happening. He replied that the committee was to decide soon. I mentioned that it would make a nice Jewish New Year's gift to hear of the success of my application because that holiday was about a week away. And per my request by *Rosh Hashanah* of 2019, I was told that my grandfather's quarter-acre block, known in Israel as one *dunam*, was in the town of Migdal, near the Sea of Galilee. I was thrilled, as I had previously thought that Grandpa's land might be in the middle of nowhere, or even in disputed territory. Researching Migdal, I found that this small town, with about 1,400 residents was the historical home of Mary Magdalene. Her name indicated her origins in Migdal. Then I found that my grandfather's plot was about a half a mile from the Sea of

Galilee, situated between two major Israeli roads that serve large parts of the country, one running north-south along the seashore, and the other east-west. It was really a good outcome.

Simultaneous to all these developments and as part of my international teaching schedule, beginning in 2015, I had been traveling to the 'general neighbourhood' of Israel almost yearly. First, I went to see my students in Turkey, and then I went twice to Cyprus, and once to Greece. In a sense, I was being prepped to visit Israel, but since I didn't know the location of Grandpa's land, I was waiting for definite information before traveling there. I hadn't been to Israel since I was twenty-one, when I worked on a *kibbutz* for three summer months.

In early 2019, however, five months before I knew the location of Grandpa's land, my angels arranged a fortuitous meeting with a special person while I was waiting to board a flight from Athens to London. Meeting this man was one of the strangest events recently. I had been travelling with a close American friend to both Cyprus and Greece. In Greece, Ann's passport was stolen in a busy train station at the start of our trip to a tourist spot four hours from Athens. I thought she might have left her passport in our Athens apartment, so I told her not to worry about it during our short trip away. She trusted my psychic sense, and we had a good trip anyway. When we returned to Athens, however, the passport was indeed missing, so I told her to call the American Embassy that evening, as, otherwise, she couldn't take the flight back to London the following Tuesday; and Monday was a Greek holiday, which I knew the American Embassy would observe. There is a telephone number in the

U.S. State Department for such emergencies, and she could organize a temporary passport that she could pick up at the Embassy the morning of our flight.

In the meantime, while Ann was dealing with this issue in Athens, I went by bus to visit a close friend in Patras, Greece for the weekend. Ann and I planned to meet at the airport check-in counter on Tuesday before our flight. Because I was nervous about missing the flight and navigating the route to the airport alone, I left early for the Athens airport Tuesday morning. When I didn't see Ann at the check-in area, I assumed that she had gone to the gate, so I continued to the gate, an hour before flight time. There was only one other person standing outside the gated area which wasn't open yet. That person was a man dressed all in black, sporting a beard and wearing a yarmulke. Recognizing our distant connections, I spoke first, asking him where he was traveling from. He replied, "Israel", at which point I continued the conversation, wondering why he was going on to London. He said that he sold real estate in Jerusalem and that he was the rabbi for a congregation east of London. When I heard about his being a real estate agent, I got excited thinking of my grandfather's land at an unknown location in northern Israel and started telling him that story. We appeared to be mutually intrigued by each other's experiences and knowledge, with him at one point showing interest in my Seraphim Blueprint teachings, which amazed me. I didn't think that a rabbi would be open to learning about such a different spiritual tradition.

When Ann appeared after others had arrived, I was still talking nonstop with the rabbi. When we boarded the full plane, the rabbi was sitting right in front of me, another coincidence, although the coincidences by then had been piling up. When we got off in London, the rabbi made a point of asking me for my business card again because he realized he had returned mine to me with his own details on the back. That seemed to indicate that he really would contact me again. Two weeks later, he called from London.

This connection continues as I write this; there have been several more unusual coincidences—because he just so happened to be moving to the States a few months later to be close to his wife's family in New Jersey, and I began instructing him in Seraphim Blueprint energies.

So, the rabbi offered to help me with my Israeli project, and when I learned of the location in Migdal, he, with his fluency in Hebrew, located the property on an Israeli map and suggested that he knew a good Israeli real estate lawyer who could help with the succession plans.

I contacted his lawyer friend in Jerusalem and started the process of getting to know him and then hiring him to assess the value of my grandfather's plot in Migdal. Initially, he thought the land was quite valuable, especially if we could change the zoning to residential. When he did the proper research, however, he saw obstacles to rezoning, which reduced the current value of the land. The monetary value of the land, or the ability to develop the land, was not important to me at this point. I was just gathering information.

My excitement levels remained high throughout all this, which was an indication to me of an unknown plan that possibly my angels, or the Seraph, had in mind. If they did have an idea for the use of this land, then, to simplify every-thing, I felt the need to see if my sister or cousins wanted to share the land and take the time and expense involved in completing the succession process. It took several months for them to come to a decision, but they agreed to let me buy them out.

At the same time, my husband and I wanted to see the land and the surrounding environment for ourselves. Ron especially wanted to go to Israel for the first time. For me, it was a return trip because I had worked on an English-speaking kibbutz in northern Israel, about 20 miles from my grandfather's land, fifty years earlier.

I started planning our trip to Israel, thinking about going there in January 2020 for about two weeks. My friend Ann suggested that it would be cheaper to stop again in London and take a separate flight to Israel. I agreed, and, also, I wanted to break up the trip because I have trouble handling long flights. Thus, I began searching for flights. Although I had been thinking that a January trip would be good, and certainly warmer than where we live in the mountains of North Carolina, the Israeli lawyer suggested that a March trip would be much more pleasant than a winter trip. So, I began planning for mid-March.

The next obstacle for traveling was where to leave our companion animals, our dog and our rabbit. We decided to leave them with a Florida friend we trusted with both. She lived quite a distance from our home, however. She had previously taken care of them while she stayed on our property, so we felt good about her caring for Bodhi and Raiyne, and thus we planned a long road trip to her and a flight to London from Orlando.

Well, the whole experience was one great test. First, getting to London, we almost missed the flight from Orlando on March 9th. We made it by one minute. I started to wonder whether we should even be on the plane. Then by the next day in London, I heard from our pet-sitter that Israel was closing its borders to all arriving Americans who would immediately be required to go into a two-week quarantine. But then, I read online there was a 72-hour grace period, so I called El Al Airlines, and they strongly suggested that we move our flight up one day, which we did.

But still, with hourly changes, we didn't know what the airline would say when we arrived at Heathrow the next day. Sure enough, at the check-in, the guy behind the counter, said, "Sorry, but if you go to Israel, you will be in a two-week quarantine and you must stay with relatives, not in a hotel." I said we couldn't do that, but had been told by an El Al agent that we could go that day to avoid the quarantine. The agent said, "Let's talk with the manager just over there". So, we all went to the manager, and I immediately told him, "We are not going to Israel as tourists, but mainly to see my grandfather's land that he purchased in Migdal 100 years ago."

The manager, said, "I am sorry, but this is the wrong time to go to Israel. Your tickets are completely refundable, or you can reschedule another trip through February of next year, with no additional cost. Besides you won't have a good time in Israel if you go now."

I looked at my husband Ron, and since this appeared to be final, we left the counter, and I said to Ron, "Let's find a place to sit down because I can't think standing up." There were no nearby empty seats, so we walked about 100 yards to a coffee kiosk inside the airport lounge, sat down, and Ron ordered hot chocolates while we talked about possible other places to go in Europe. We finished our hot chocolates, but still hadn't reached any conclusions, when, suddenly, I saw in the distance the El Al manager walking slowly in our direction. How he knew where we were is a total mystery. When he got to us, he said, "I called Border Security in Israel, and they are making an exception in your case. You can fly on this El Al flight without going into quarantine in Israel." He couldn't even see us from the El Al counter before approaching us. It felt completely like Seraphic support. I was ecstatic.

This is how I knew the Seraph was part of the process. This one event confirmed for me that the laborious lengths that I had gone to the previous year might have a higher purpose. I started to relax about all the restrictions we were facing as the world began to lock down, first in Israel where, on day three of our two-week stay, all Israeli restaurants and hotels closed. But we weren't staying in hotels, just in private apartments, and a week on, in a *kibbutz*. The rental car agency didn't lock us out, and the *kibbutz*, near Migdal, welcomed us at first, confused by the new directives, and then, by the next morning, let us know we could stay the week we had reserved and that they would also serve us breakfast. Next, its leaders became interested in hearing more about the Seraphim Blueprint, and with no other tourists to host, three *Kibbutzniks* took Seraphim Healing (Level 1) with me while we were there. These three were the first in Israel to learn Seraphim Blueprint.

Every day, we witnessed a miraculous, unique aspect to our trip. The weather was glorious for our first view of Grandpa's plot, and there was a huge, stately escarpment just across the road because the town of Migdal is within the Great Rift Valley that stretches all the way into the heart of Africa. The Sea of Galilee and its surroundings are 700 feet below sea level, which gives it a tropical, wet winter climate, and a hot dry summer climate. Nearby, lush green fields had commercial mango trees, which gave me an idea of what can be grown on Grandpa's land.

Our last five nights in Israel were in Jerusalem. I wanted to go to the Western Wall of the Second Temple, the last wall still standing. Israeli Security officers stationed near the Temple were puzzled by how two Americans could be touring Israel when all tourists were forbidden to travel while there. On our first attempt, they wouldn't let us approach this holy of holies. A few days later, however, we found security officials at a different entrance gate to Jerusalem's old city, who didn't question us, so we entered there, and I felt the ecstasy and power of touching the ancient Temple wall. A day before, Ron had walked right into Christ's inner tomb, at the Church of the Holy Sepulchre, which was completely empty, so that he could spend a half an hour alone soaking up the spiritual energies. When we returned to America, I read that the day after Ron's visit there (March 25, 2020), the Israeli government closed the church to all visitors for the first time in 671 years! It stayed closed for two months.

Although many people worldwide were experiencing travel interruptions of all kinds, our original return flight plans held as further proof of angelic support. Maharishi Mahesh Yogi, my first spiritual mentor, often spoke of "Nature Support", which he claimed was Nature's way of letting us know we were doing what was right, or were on the true path. He said Nature would smooth the way for our endeavours to the point that we couldn't ignore all the coincidences that were occurring. Several times in my life, I have witnessed such support, which others might call "being in the flow" or "being in the zone". When working full-time for a spiritual cause, it becomes an obvious phenomenon, but when halfway in the spiritual realms and halfway in the material realms, as it was with Grandpa's plot, it is less obvious. For me to feel this special support, it appears to have been necessary to step out of my normal daily routine and take up a new challenge, one that came from a totally unexpected source, from a long-deceased ancestor, who himself broke out of his own boundaries in the early 1920s to take a stand in a far-off land that I don't believe he ever saw.

Ruth Rendely is a meditation instructor, healer, and spiritual teacher. Partnering with a Seraph for the past 25 years, she has revived a spiritual system, now known as Seraphim Blueprint, and has trained teachers of this system worldwide.

All Those Angels, Really?

We were a whole bunch of us, all together in this beautiful location, just enjoying each other's company, unaware of any conflicts or problems to be solved—a sort of blissful environment, when a beautiful angel showed up and asked for attention.

"Well, there are problems on Earth, and we are looking for volunteers", she said. "Yes, you will have to incarnate, be born again and go through the whole process of becoming human."

There was silence. We were all very serious. Being born again. Repeat this whole painful process of making mistakes, enduring pain, frustration, disappointment, despair...

But this angel was so beautiful. She had a warm glow around her, emanating confidence and support. "Well, any volunteers?" she repeated.

Somebody asked, "What is the mission? Could you explain it a bit?"

"It's very important. There is again a war on Earth. We need a bunch of souls to bring light into this terrible destructive darkness."

We all looked at each other, devastated. Slowly some of us entities got up and gathered around the angel. After a bit of hesitation, I joined those brave souls. One by one, the angel gave assignments. I was appointed to incarnate in Oudenaarde, a small Belgian town, to become the newest little sister in a family of three children.

With a bit of a squeaky thought that barely left my soul, I asked: "What do I need to do, what is my assignment?"

"Be the Light".

It turned out that all of us received the same order and were sent to different destinations on Earth.

Mama Blanche became pregnant with me, the baby who developed as a girl. For eight months, my mama was crying. She did not want another child. There was no food. She did not know how to feed her three children, her husband, her father Papa Richard to begin with. How was she going to fill another mouth? She had to stand in long lines with food vouchers for milk, for bread, for eggs, if there was anything available at all by the time it was your turn. And as her belly grew, and neighbors became aware of her pregnancy, she got criticized, laughed at, scolded. Bernard, my father, had his own very good reasons to want a fourth child.

The year was 1943. Belgium was occupied by the German army. The Nazis claimed all available food for their soldiers in the occupied territories. Hitler had now invaded Poland, Czechoslovakia, the Netherlands, France, and Belgium. He had the ill-inspired ambition to attack Russia. Of course, there are not enough German workers to continue production of weapons or necessary material to sustain his war effort in Germany. In all occupied territories, the mandate went out that "All men between the age of 16 and 36 will work in German factories, except the fathers of four children."

My father, Bernard Bral, was part of the Resistance in

this town of Oudenaarde. His entire family was involved in this dangerous, clandestine operation. Through his contacts with the Belgian Government in Exile in London, he knew all the maneuvers and troop advancements. He knew that Churchill had convinced the American President, Roosevelt, to "Join the War Theater", that the Allies were advancing from Italy, and that they had already devastated the German occupation in North Africa.

My family would provide a safe-haven to pilots who had been shot down—and survived—through a carefully constructed network of members. My great-aunt, "Tante" Irene Van den Heule, the youngest sister of my grandmother Stephanie, was the gardener of Baron Liefmans. She and her husband, Uncle Ivo, lived in the cottage of the Baron's Mansion. Great-Uncle Ivo worked in Baron Liefmans' brewery. Workers at the time were dressed in "overalls", a simple jumpsuit with the name of the brewery embroidered on the upper breast pocket. My father directed the Allied pilots from wherever they had been rescued to Aunt Irene's cottage at night.

Dressed in the brewery's overalls, she walked the pilots from her garden cottage to St. Elizabeth's Hospital under the nose of the omnipresent Nazis whose motto was "Ordnung Soll Sein", meaning, "Order Must Be", and they posed as a couple of love-struck youngsters. Mother Superior of the hospital would work her contacts to direct English, or Canadian pilots safely towards France. The hospital was located close to the River Schelde. This was one of the escape routes during the darkness of night.

Unfortunately, my father, Louis Bernard Bral, was ambushed and killed on the dark, rainy and stormy evening of December 18, 1943. He owned and operated the only garage in Oudenaarde.

A phone call had come, telling him that he had to deliver the truck, which had been repaired that day, to the fruit hall that evening. So, he did. Then he rode his bike from the delivery place to our home. The road was along the River Schelde. There were mandatory blackouts. Nobody was allowed visible lights on the streets. Even in all the houses, families had to cover windows, so no light could shine into the streets; this was to protect the locations of cities from bombers at night.

I was born early October that same year. I never knew my father. As I was growing up, we did not celebrate Christmas. It was too painful for Mama. Yet, everyone in this small town had known Bernard Bral and our family's history. As a child, I believed that the world was a friendly, lovely place. Everybody was so friendly and kind to me and my family.

Many years later, my husband, daughters and grandchildren were on vacation in Crested Butte, Colorado. We took a two-day horse trip through the wilderness, with overnight lodging. After a long and beautiful ride up and down the mountains, approaching the cabana at the bottom of a hill, my horse got excited and, instead of holding her tight, I let her run down the hill. Unfortunately, the earth was moist and soft after the rain. She lost her balance and fell. I jumped and did not get crushed underneath her beautiful heavy body. I quickly got up and calmed her down. I did not break anything—a miracle really—but had the mother of all bruises over my entire body. Returning the next day on the lovely horse was a rather painful experience.

Back in town, I went to see a healer and asked her to do

her magic over me. After the session, she told me, "Something incredible happened. As soon as I started moving my hands over your body, fourteen angels filled the room. I have never seen this happen before". Hmm, I thought, how interesting. When I was a little girl, I had to go to my grandmother Bonne-Maman Stephany after school. Mama Blanche, now a widow with four children, had to work long hours. I could only return home on Sundays. Every night, Grandma Stephany and I recited the same prayer: "S'avonds als ik slapen ga, veertien Engelen komen mij na". (Evenings when I go to sleep, fourteen Angels come with me). Turns out that this prayer is a song from the opera "Hansel and Gretel" by Humperdinck, as I discovered later in life, to keep the children safe in the woods, as they forage for food. Fourteen angels!

One day in 2005, as I was living in San Francisco, an email arrived in my inbox from a certain Ruth Rendely about a seminar involving a Seraph. So, intrigued, I signed up. That same evening, I encountered Alex Brandin, also European with an accent, born in East Germany and intrigued by this angel topic. I ended up taking all Ruth's Seraphim courses, becoming a teacher, and, through Alex, a Guardian of Gaia. We are creating and helping to maintain crystals, spread out over our beautiful Mother Earth, to protect and guard her from the devastating abuses our human race has, unconsciously, succeeded in inflicting on her. Now, we are sending love, light, consciousness and energy worldwide, wherever we are called to do so.

So, from when I was born and throughout my entire life, it appears that angels have been my companions. All those angels, really! They surely know what they are doing. Amazing and very humbling for us humans.

Rita M. Bral, BA, MA, AP graduated from the University of Gent, Belgium, with a BA in Art History, with an MA in Romance Languages and an AP in Pedagogy. Currently, she works for Software Research, Inc. as VP of Corporate Communications. She held the mandate of Honorary Consul of Belgium for Northern California and Nevada from 1993-2013. In recognition of her services to the Belgian government, HRH King Albert II knighted her twice, first as "Knight of the Crown" and later as "Knight in the Order of Léopold". She serves on the boards of different Bay Area organizations, including "Education Francophone Bay Area" and "The Institute for European Studies" at U.C. Berkeley.

Slimy Angels on the Walkway

Sometimes angels come in the form of slugs. Or snails. Or both.

January 29. 2018

I am being held captive in a house, although I am allowed to swim. There is a lap pool attached to the house, where I can swim daily. But when I swim there, I am attached to a man. He swims on top of me. We swim together. With his help, I can swim faster and stronger. He helps propel me forward. But he is on top of me. Still, I am content.

But one day, he tries to kill me. He has a set of knives in a box with a latch, and he takes out a knife and tries to stab me. I escape and run to a house next door, where I stay, waiting. I order dehydrated fruits, and that is how I survive while I wait. Until one day, I receive a package of chocolates. I am reunited with the swimmer man, and we swim off together in total balance.

I wake up.

Before I get out of bed, I write down this dream—which I entitle "My hermaphrodite, synchronized swimmer dream"—in my dream journal and start my day. The image of me, both male and female, swimming along gracefully, gliding along the water, remains with me as I prepare the kids' sandwiches for school and as I go about my morning routine. It is such a peaceful image that it gives me a sense of calm as I complete work deadlines and household chores.

As soon as I have a chance, I work the dream. By this, I mean that I write in my journal, speaking from the various elements of the dream—the houses, the knife, the dried fruit, and the chocolate—which mirror aspects of my own unconscious. This method of "Dream Work" is based on the idea that the images we create while sleeping are a window to our soul, the key to understanding ourselves beneath the surface of our waking thoughts and feelings.

When I have this dream, I am at a crossroads in my life, a point at which I am craving freedom to break away from the religious rules and systems I tried hard to contort myself to since my modern orthodox Jewish childhood—whether by being stricter than my parents to be more "authentic," or by becoming an orthodox feminist and trying to change the system from within, or by breaking away from orthodoxy but still clinging to classical Jewish law.

When I give voice to the houses, they tell me I am my own captor and that I have two sides—or aspects—of myself—the anima and animus, female and male, which I keep compartmentalized rather than breaking down the walls and uniting them harmoniously.

The knife tells me it tried to kill my anima (feminine side) when I fought for women's equal access in a male-created system, rather than advocate for a more radical revamping of the system that would bring anima and animus into balance. I am thankful that I escaped just in time.

The dried fruit tells me it can keep me alive while I am in this liminal time of waiting but barely because it lacks the vivacity I need to truly *feel* alive. The chocolates are a peace offering inviting me to come back and incorporate my masculine side rather than kill it off.

But I do not know how to move forward. I am afraid to let go of the boundaries that have been such an integral part of my identity, of who I always thought I was. Can I still be me without these frameworks? Can I let go of them entirely, not even using them to measure myself or break away from? Who, I wonder, is the *me* without those boundaries? If I get to the other side of the border, will I still exist at all?

For days, I walk around with the energy of this dream, knowing it is a significant one in my life, knowing there is a message for me there, knowing that it holds the key to how to find that kind of peaceful balance in my life I experienced at the end of my dream; but I do not know what the message is.

At the same time, slugs start showing up in my life in surprising ways. I was told angels appear at the crossroads, but no one warned me they could appear in the form of a slug.

First, I notice them hanging around my one-lane naturally filtered lap pool. I swim backstroke, for example, and see a slug moving along the wall, leaving a residue behind her, as slugs do. There are many of them. Every day, I see more and more. But it is winter in Galilee, which is slug season. So, I am not alarmed.

Then I step on one. I am walking on my patio towards the pool, barefoot, as I always do, and am startled by the gooey feeling beneath my big toe. Yuck! I crush the poor thing, and it becomes, instantly, a puddle of water before my eyes.

I am curious, especially when I get into the pool to swim and see what could be three of these slugs' babies moving along the edge of the pool. But once I finish swimming, I put the slugs out of my mind.

That night, I awake to the feel of something slimy on my finger. I turn on the light, bring my hand to my eyes and am shocked to find a slug on my hand. Now that is too much. I shake the slug off and do my best to fall back to sleep, but it is no use. Besides, the slug is still slithering along my bedroom floor.

I get out of bed, pick up the slug with a tissue, and put it outside. But there is no use trying to go back to sleep. It is already 5:30 A.M., and the kids will have to be woken soon, anyway; so, I go to my computer and do a search for "slugs" on the internet. Perhaps there I will find the explanation for why they are showing up for me here and now, at the crossroads.

I already know something about slugs. For example, slugs move slowly, like me. We both have no choice. It is how we are built. I live with a degenerative genetic muscular disease, a form of muscular dystrophy called FSHD. Slugs move through a muscular contraction of what is called their one "foot", which moves them along. Because I have foot drop in both of my legs, I cannot lift my toes, so my feet also slide along the floor when I walk, which is why I trip often.

I click on a link to an online entry about slugs. A slug is almost all water, I read. It is therefore always in need of water, which is why it has a protective mucus it leaves behind as it moves. The mucus is a liquid crystal, a unique and amazing substance that attracts water and therefore keeps the slug hydrated. It also helps the slug move along surfaces and helps slugs find one another.

Like the dried fruit in my dream, I feel dried out when I am not in water. I swim daily, spending at least two hours a day in the pool, the place I can move my muscles with the most ease. Yet, with an annoying condition called "dry mouth"—a symptom of the FSHD, since I can only close my mouth with effort and concentration—even that is not enough.

A slug must be careful to remain hydrated. But rather than rely on water from the outside, it creates its own liquid crystal to keep it from drying out. What is my liquid crystal that keeps me hydrated and that I leave behind me in my wake so others can find me? My writing, my actions in the world, my meaningful interactions with others…

Slugs are hermaphrodites. They are both male and female. Slugs have managed to do what many of us aspire to do—balance our male and female sides, our anima and animus, in a healthy way. Like the swimmer in my dream.

Slugs have a collective history. They were once mollusks but have shed their shell. What we are seeing is an animal that has broken free of boundaries. Now that is a description to which I can relate. It took me years to stop trying to fit into the shell of Orthodox Judaism.

Yet, I am afraid to let go completely of my shell. Will I not fall apart with any clear boundaries set from outside myself? I fear melting, like the Wicked Witch of the West in the Wizard of Oz, into a pool of goo, not unlike a slug. And so, here I sit, at the crossroads, unable to move forward.

Slug has found a way to stay together, to remain whole, and to not melt away, even without outer boundaries. What is her secret?

When the kids are off to school and Jacob is off to work, I go out to the pool for my daily swim. I am not at all surprised to find Slug waiting for me. But this time, I pay attention. If Slug is me, my life, my dreams, I will feel into Slug's energy to try and discern her message to me.

I stand in the water and watch Slug moving along at her slow pace, leaving her liquid crystal mucus behind her. I put my face right up to her, so I can see her in detail, in her full slug glory.

She is truly beautiful. Shiny and smooth. Gracefully moving forward, feeling her way with her tentacles. Yes, I read that on the internet. Slugs don't see or think, they feel. That is how they move forward.

Slug does not need her shell. But what prevents her from melting away? Slug does have a remnant of a shell, but it is an internal shell that keeps her together. That too I read. That is her secret.

There is nothing wrong with boundaries. In fact, they are a necessary part of life if they are a sincere expression of what your soul needs, and if they are not an expression of what your waking self has convinced you that you need to fit into society or please others—while your soul shrivels away from lack of hydration.

I watch Slug in a meditative state for a time not measured in human terms. Then I hear Slug's message: Feel your way forward. *Feel your way forward. Feel your way forward. You are my sister now, Dreamer. You are free of your shell. You are water. You are anima and animus. You have your own inner shell. Listen to your inner voice, trust in your heart, and feel your way forward.*

I start to swim, with Slug's message going through my head like a mantra. *Feel your way forward. Feel your way forward.* I become the energy of my dream. A slug, feeling my way forward with inner peace.

APRIL 27, 2020

We are amid a global pandemic, and I have been sheltering in place at home—which is in a tiny kibbutz in Galilee—with Jacob and six of our seven children, ranging in age from 9 to 24. The oldest lives in Haifa and is sheltering in place with her partner there.

Because my FSHD affects various of my muscles, including those involved with breathing, my doctor advised me not to leave the house and to minimize, as much as possible, contact with others.

I have been frightened of contracting the virus, but I have felt safe enough, since the government's restrictions limited my family's goings-and-comings and mixing with others. But as soon as Passover ended, the government began talking about lifting the restrictions; and this week this plan went into effect.

Is now really the time to be easing up the restrictions? So long as there is no vaccine for COVID-19, why wouldn't the virus simply start spreading as quickly as it was before, I ask myself. And if it does, can an entire country be reined back in, once it has been let loose after being confined for this long?

These questions have been on my mind and heart since

Passover ended and cabin fever has been in the air. This is just when snails start to show up in my life in abundant and unusual ways.

Since meeting Slug the year before, I not only keep a journal of dreams I remember when waking, but I also pay attention to the natural world. Whether we call it God, our higher self, our unconscious, or our inner voice, there is communication from a deeper and/or higher place when we dream, as well as when we open ourselves to the wonders of the natural world.

We dream several times a night, but we only remember some; even within those dreams, only certain images stick with us. Similarly, I have learned, there is so much surrounding us, but only certain phenomena catch our eyes at specific times. If we lean into those dreams and waking elements that demand our attention, there are messages for us there.

The natural world is God's—or the Spirit of the Universe's—dreamscape in which we—humans, plants and animals alike—connect and play a part. If God can speak to us in dreams (as is written in Numbers 12:6) why not through Creation? Like with an especially vivid or recurring dream calling out to be understood, Snail, like Slug, is calling for me to take notice, and it is up to me to observe, listen and try to understand.

First, it is the snails who appear one day on the walls of my swimming lane, where the slugs appeared two years before. Tens of them, in all shapes and sizes. I swim back and forth, watching Snail and trying to discern her message to me. But it is not clear.

Then my daughter, who is an artist and is home from the

army, comes to me with a series of snail drawings she has been working on, inspired by the lockdown: renditions of people sheltering in place in their own private snail shells, each looking self-contained and content in their isolated solitude.

Later that day, my youngest daughter comes to me with a lemon-sized snail shell in her hand. She says she found it in our dog's mouth and that she suspected the dog had eaten the snail. Then, guess what I find in my mouth that night while eating my salad at dinner: a tiny snail.

Is Snail trying to warn me? *There is still danger out there. Don't be seduced into thinking this is over. Don't be lured into coming out of your shell too soon.*

The next day, my older daughter, who has gone back to the army, sends me a new addition to her snail series. It is of a backpacker, with a snail shell in lieu of a knapsack, looking back into the horizon. Like a recurring dream that does not stop coming until you pay attention, Snail is not going to leave me alone until I hear her message loud and clear.

This drawing evokes for me Bohemian Woman who appeared to me first in a dream, with a knapsack on her back, chanting, "I once had a head, I once had a head," as she walks off into the horizon. She lives in a loft which I visit in my dream after she has already left for an adventure. It is filled with costume jewelry.

When I worked the dream, I understood her message: *live more from the heart, less from the head.* Bohemian Woman is the free spirit in me. Slug, feeling her way forward—from the heart, not the head. Yet, even Bohemian Woman has a home she goes back to, with treasures whose value can be measured only by her.

Now, here she is appearing to me with a shell on her back instead of a pack. *There are times when an inner shell is not enough, she is telling me. There are times when you need to let your head set boundaries to what your heart desires. And there are times when even the most free of spirits needs to head home, lie low and hunker down with her personal inner treasures.*

As much as I would like to go back to my life as it was, I, personally, will not be rushing out of my shell. In fact, as others rush out of their shells, I may need to retreat even further back into my own.

* * *

August 2, 2020

It is hot, and there is no relief in sight. Numbers of serious COVID-19 cases in Israel are rising, as are the numbers of deaths from the virus. Even if a vaccine is created, it may take years for it to be developed and tested safely and ethically. People are pouring out into the streets to protest. I too am frustrated. The government has not handled this pandemic well, although it is not clear what handling it well would look like.

Besides, I am still not venturing out except in ways that feel moderately safe. I am doing my best to remain physically within my shell, while allowing my soul to soar free and not feel confined by the physical protections that feel wise now in this new reality.

I need both Slug and Snail to move forward in these challenging times. Yet, I do not feel at peace. I feel in danger now, not of melting away, but of drying out.

The kids are all off from school now, and we have a whole month until even online learning begins again. Just one hot and endless day after another to fill with our anxieties and despair.

We venture out to the sea shore and try to find a place with few others around to spread our sheet and sit down. Jacob heads to the water with the kids, but as much as water is my element, I am afraid to go in with others around us doing the same. I do not want to be too close to anyone with the virus in the air.

I decide to take a walk further down the beach where there is no lifeguard and therefore fewer people. I walk, trying to keep my balance because walking is difficult enough for me on even firm ground. Luckily, I am wearing my walking aids and have my walking sticks with me to keep me from falling.

And then I see it: a large conch shell the size of my foot. I lean over and pick it up. It is empty, yet beautiful. This is not a usual find on this beach. It is calling out for my attention. Snail has left, gone on to her next place, leaving her shell behind for me to find.

I recall Slug's liquid crystal, what it, too, leaves in its wake, as it keeps itself hydrated to stay alive. The thought of what I would leave behind—my mark on the world—gave me comfort back then.

But if the world is coming to an end, even that feels empty—like this shell. If this shell is the Third Coming from my poem, what is the message it holds for me?

I remember a fragment from a dream I had the night before:

I am writing on a computer and feel anxious that I need to get it all into the computer before there is a power outage and all is lost.

While looking at the empty shell in my hand, I feel the computer screen speaking to me through this shell:

I, the computer, am not afraid. It is the dreamer who is afraid that what she is writing will be erased if there is a power outage before she gets all her thoughts into me. But I know that her words won't be lost, because it is all in my memory. Even if there is a power outage, her writings will be saved. Only if there is an end to everything, to the world as we know it, will they be lost. But then everything will be gone, including me, so it won't matter.

Dreamer, you have nothing to fear. Your writing will be preserved, your messages to the world will be heard, and you will be able to communicate through your words and stories.

When you die, your writings will live on. And once you are gone, you might not even care anymore because you will be in a different realm like this snail that left its shell. You will be Spirit, united with the One.

And if the world as we know it ceases to exist, it will not matter anymore if your words are lost. Nothing will matter. Or all will matter. But nothing will be as it was, so there is no reason to fear losing your own personal achievements or contributions. That is all ego which will be gone, melted away like the slug I crushed with my foot.

So, dreamer: Relax. Be present. Do your best. And trust.

And so, I add to my list of angels who appear to me at the crossroads, Shell. Sometimes angels appear in the form of a slug. Or a snail. Or a shell. And, sometimes, all three.

Dr. Haviva Ner-David is a rabbi, writer, and social activist. She is the founding rabbinic chairperson of *Shmaya: A Mikveh for Mind, Body and Soul,* where she officiates and creates full body water immersion ceremonies and runs workshops for visiting groups. She is the author of two published spiritual journey memoirs, with a third on the way. She lives on Kibbutz Hannaton in Israel's Galilee with her life partner, Jacob, and their seven children.

Two Jewish Tales
with a Twist

Life in the Big City

This is the story of a demon named Pushnik, who stalked the Lower East Side in the early years of the 20th century. Pushnik was no ordinary demon, but a middle-ranking devil of the second order, a venerable and respected figure in all the major diabolical societies; for demons have their own fraternal organizations just as angels and humans do.

Most demons do not stay with the same population, but as all his colleagues knew, Pushnik had a way with Jews, right from the very beginning. He'd trained under the devil that tempted Cain to kill his brother Abel, and several centuries later it was he who incited the Israelites to rise against the Assyrians, the Babylonians, and then the Romans, each time with tragic consequences. And during our long years of exile, from Spain all the way to China, whenever Jews came together in community, it was he who created discord. In each of those different eras he appeared in a slightly different form and was known by a different name. It was only toward the end of the nineteenth century that he started calling himself Pushnik, and it's by that moniker that he has been known ever since.

Pushnik had been happy working in the dark forests of Eastern Europe. He worked there for years. But his delight at coming to the carnal and polluted city of New York was almost limitless when his constituents began their long removal, and he followed them there. Rather than having to wander from village to dirty little village, all of them dark, and none of them even half so romantic as anything from "Fiddler on the Roof," Pushnik could spend his time sitting in a single cafeteria, eating and smoking cigarettes. And without getting up so much as to go to the bathroom, which of course he didn't have to do, he could corrupt in half a day of talking more Jews than he would have been able to reach in Europe in an entire year. Yes, for Pushnik, if you will allow me to play with words in this fashion, for Pushnik—New York was heaven on Earth—a demon's paradise.

From the time that he first arrived in the New World, Pushnik assumed a variety of disguises, all of which allowed him to do the greatest evil by rubbing shoulders not just with those who were inclined in his direction, but also with those in search of the highest good. He worked as a prostitute and then as a physician, as a schoolteacher and then a petty gangster. But, over time, he settled upon one materialization that allowed him to do his corrupting work most effectively. He posed as the head of a garment worker's organization, one that shall remain unnamed.

"What a city!" he liked to tell the men and women who belonged to the organization he headed, as they sat together in his favorite cafeteria, smoking and eating. "Only in America! Every opportunity! You should try the fish. In fact, try anything. Go ahead. It's on me." And from such innocence, such utter delight in this new land, how many

Jews under Pushnik's tutelage went from lox to lobster, all in a matter of weeks? In truth, I cannot tell you. Those records are sealed for the next two thousand years. But I do not exaggerate when I say they number in the thousands, the tens of thousands. In fact, no other demon has ever been so successful in tempting the evil impulses in his clients as Pushnik was in those not so long ago rough and tumble years.

In 1928, there was a big conference of demons held in New York City, in the cellar of a rundown hotel amid what used to be called Hell's Kitchen, since gentrified and now called Clinton. At a time when all of God's local angels were preparing for the Great Stock Market Crash, still a year away, the demons were so confident of the immediate results of their disastrous work in creating it that they gathered together to make long-range plans. Long before anyone else imagined it, they were concocting a Second World War, plotting gas chambers, death camps, nuclear disasters, global pollution, and even creating goal sheets for the distant post-war era and for possible climate extinction. And it was there, at that meeting that Pushnik laid out his most successful plan.

"Listen," he said, in the gravelly voice that had become his trademark, "we're going to win the next war. We all know that. These humans think it's a matter of which of their sides wins. They think war is a battle between good and evil. But we all know better than that. War is always evil, and whichever of their sides wins, the victory will be ours!" Here Pushnik's colleagues cheered, for they had worked hard to convince their human clients that war did matter, in precisely the ways that would best serve their own nefarious agenda. But for Pushnik that was only the beginning.

"Here amid these bald mountains," Pushnik went on to

say (an allusion to the skyscrapers of his time, that would soon be dwarfed by even vaster shadow-casting structures, and an allusion to the shiny top of his own big head, which brought laughs to everyone gathered). "I guarantee that by the year 1959, you will see among my constituents, if not amongst all humanity, a culture of barren values, vulgar material obsessions, and a numbing pornography of thought that will cripple their offspring for the next five generations."

The demons packed into that dark and narrow basement room burst into thunderous applause. After it faded, Pushnik laid out his plan, the way that he was going to subvert his Jews, to get them to surrender to the evil impulse. All around the room you could hear the scratch, scratch, scratch of pencils on paper, as Italian, Irish, Polish, German, Danish, Negro (pardon the word, it was the one they used then), and all other demonic advocates, were writing down the essentials of Pushnik's plan, translating it into the psychological temptations best suited to their own populations.

"By 1979," he added, "the grandchildren of the humble citizens we see about us, wretched, poor, downtrodden, will be wearing jewels and fur coats, killing just like everyone else, buying shares in multi-national corporations, and polluting the world for the next ten thousand years. If our work is successful, and we know it will be, they will survive one disaster, only to create another one themselves, in what at first seems to be their salvation." Again, a sulfurous applause filled the low-ceilinged room. "And," Pushnik concluded, "by the year 1999, my Jews, in fact all of humanity will be living in a state of moral bankruptcy that will make next year's little financial adventure seem like a pretty little butterfly caught on sticky fly paper."

Naturally, or perhaps we might better say, unnaturally, all of this came to pass, exactly as Pushnik had outlined. Highly pleased with his work on our planet, Asmodeus, the chief of all the demons, raised him to the top of his order and allowed him to retire with a very large pension to a lush uninhabited planet in the Valmindrax Galaxy where he has been working, uninterrupted, on his memoirs.

The Rabbi's Wife

They took all the villagers out to a ravine at the edge of town. They lined them up and shot them, then quickly shoveled a layer of dirt over their bodies, including those who were bloody and wounded but still alive.

Had you been able to see this scene with other eyes, you would have known that one by one, fluttering down in soft rosy pink robes, the very angels who had guided each soul from heaven down to earth when it was born were there to take each dying soul in their arms and carry them back up to heaven.

Reb Mendel, the rabbi of this little village, died with the words of the *Shema* on his lips. Standing beside him, her kerchief flapping in the wind, his wife Leah Sarah stood with one hand raised in a fist. Her final act of life—to spit at the line of soldiers facing her, most of them young enough to be her grandchildren.

Had you been able to see this scene with those other eyes, you would have noticed Reb Mendel's guiding angel coming to him with open arms, stroking his cheek, pressing the softest of heavenly lips to his bloody brow, and lifting him up from his gray and mangled corpse. And had you looked two feet away, to the body of his loyal wife Leah Sarah, lying crumpled and bloody in the ravine, her legs bent under her, her kerchief torn off, you would have seen her own most loving angel kneeling in the dirt beside her.

Leah Sarah saw the angel winging down, through dusty, weary eyes, with her last breath. And, as the angel bent to lift her in its loving arms, she turned to it and said, "Don't you dare to lay a hand on me!" And so it was, with Leah Sarah kicking and struggling, screaming as never had any of its charges screamed before, that Leah Sarah's angel rose up through clouds toward the firmament.

Through gates of sparkling gold and colors they had not seen since the last time they were there, the souls of the dead arrived in heaven, cradled in the strong arms of their guiding angels. Some were crying, others were awestruck, for when we are born we forget the light, forget the splendor. Our eyes are tuned to other sights, to other wonders. Several were singing out, others were praying. Only Leah Sarah was yelling, much to the embarrassment of her angel. "Put me down!" she cried. "Let me go! I don't want to be here!"

Now, the souls of the dead are like newborn babies, weak and wobbly. At least they usually are. So, Leah Sarah's angel was afraid to put her down. Fortunately, it was a strong angel, for she was still kicking and screaming as it carried her off from the others, not wanting to upset them. Reb Mendel called out to her, but his words were lost in her protestations.

Desperate, not knowing what to do, her angel sought out its superior angel, Mattathias. This angel's domain was just on the borders between second and third heaven, a place that newly dead souls rarely get to, unless they are saints. But Leah Sarah's angel didn't know what else to do. In millions of years of being a celestial guide for multiple planets, nothing like this had ever happened to it before.

Thank God, that Mattathias was there when the two of them arrived. If angels could get black and blue, poor Leah Sarah's angel would have been a mess.

Most humans, seeing so bright a being as Mattathias would have bowed or bent or averted their eyes. But not Leah Sarah. She just snapped, "Put me down!" Which her angel did when Mattathias nodded at it.

"What have we here?" Mattathias said, in a voice so honey-glad and golden that most souls would melt into blissful tears. But not Leah Sarah. "What kind of crap is this?" she demanded. "I'm born into a dirty little village. Married off to a pious husband who can never give me children. We scrape and struggle like the rest of our kind. Afraid, afraid always, cowering from life. And then, when I die, no, when I'm slaughtered, on the edge of the filthy ravine where we throw our scraps of garbage, you send a smiling angel to get me and bring me here. Why?" she snapped, "Do you expect me to be grateful?" she added, with a leer.

Leah Sarah's angel was distressed, dismayed, and felt responsible. Perhaps the guidance it had offered Leah Sarah in dreams and whispered messages throughout her life had not been adequate. So, it turned to her and said, "But all that is over now, Leah Sarah. You are here with us in heaven."

"Heaven," she snapped back at him. "Over! You think that I can forget a life and death like that? A line of soldiers with their rifles! You're worse than they are. They were done with me the moment I was dead. But you, you continue to torture me."

Bowing, just a tiny little bit, her angel looked up at her and said, "But Leah Sarah, this is a place of blessings. Of joy, forgiveness, and comfort."

Turning with fury in her eyes, Leah Sarah spit at her angel's feet. Although the spit vanished immediately, the feel of the spray remained with the angel for eons, hot and burning. Then Leah Sarah looked around at the halls, the light, the beauty and let out a bellowing "No!" the fury of which shook every wall in the first, second, and third heaven. "No!" she shouted again. "No! There is no way that I am ever going to forgive you, any of you," she said, looking up toward seventh heaven.

Jaw clenched, her hands raised in fists, Leah Sarah turned to the angels and said, "This makes me sick. There are things you cannot make better. Not by blessings and not by this," she intoned, waving her hand over her head, to encompass everything she saw.

"But..." her angel said. Only to be cut off by Mattathias.

Sparkling gold and emerald, Mattathias turned to Leah Sarah and said calmly, "You are right." At those words, her own angel slumped, the wind knocked out of its wings. And even Leah Sarah changed, grew quiet, not expecting such an answer.

"I'm right?" she asked, those defiant shoulders now collapsed.

And Mattathias nodded back to her. "Yes." Her angel's wings began to flit and flutter. It didn't know what to do. Finally, Mattathias broke the silence by saying, "Yes, Leah Sarah, you are right. But what can we do?"

Here, the fury rose in her again. "What kind of God would make a world like that?"

"Leah Sarah, Leah Sarah," Mattathias said, sounding too much like her husband to endear her to it. "Leah Sarah.

When God made you humans, It made you with free will. Not even the wiser and far more loving whales and the dolphins of your world have that." Leah Sarah snorted. Having never seen an ocean, a sea, or even a large river, dolphins and whales meant nothing to her, and the old tale of Jonah was far from her mind.

Mattathias began again, by asking her a question. "And so, tell me Leah Sarah - given everything, would you rather have been made without free will?"

Hands on her hips, Leah Sarah stood there biting the inside of her left cheek, a habit that always annoyed her husband. Finally, she looked back at the two angels, one vaster and more luminous than the other and said, "All right. But what good is free will when there are people like those down there?" And she pointed an arthritic finger back down toward the earth, which they could see beneath them like a faint blue pearl.

"I cannot answer that," said Mattathias, "Except to invite you to go back. To go back and try to make it different. Different, and better." And so it was, not too much later (in heaven's time) that our same guiding angel stood with folded yellow wings in the delivery room of a crowded hospital in a dense and noisy section of the city of New York, as a little baby slipped out of its mother's struggling body and into the world again. Screaming.

"Listen to the lungs on this one," Dr. Ginzburg said to Ms. Leavitt, the nurse, who was holding the infant in her competent, bloody, wet, hands. "She's gonna be one tough little girl," Dr. Ginzburg added. And, she is, our little Tiffany. Tiffany Steinberg-Greenberg. Come back Jewish again.

Andrew Ramer is the author of *Queering the Text: Biblical, Medieval, and Modern Jewish Stories; Torah Told Different; Deathless: The Complete, Uncensored, Heartbreaking, and Amazing Autobiography of Serach bat Asher, the Oldest Woman in the World, and Fragments of the Brooklyn Talmud.* He is the world's first ordained interfaith *maggid* (sacred storyteller); many of his blessings and prayers appear in the feminist prayer book of Congregation Sha'ar ZahavDra in San Francisco. He lives in Oakland, California.

Seraphim Miracles

There are many stories about angels. Even as a child, I placed angels at the center of my world. Some extraordinary events are evidence of their existence. At this point, I want to share a personal story that occurred years ago.

While my son was studying in high school, he wanted to continue with a university education outside of Turkey. He had decided on engineering sciences, and was accepted to several universities in the United States. It was great to see him happy at the end of his efforts. My husband and I were happy for him. The week he finished his studies, he got accepted by an engineering construction company in our country. After his pre-internship ended, he came home and told me he would never be an engineer. He gave up an engineering career at that point. I did not expect this. I tried to be calm and asked him what he wanted to do. He told me he had decided to study at a medical school in Europe. After he had attended four years of university, with mostly engineering courses, as well as similar courses in high school, he wasn't prepared for a medical education. I felt a brief despair, but an inner voice was telling me "Relax, be of good cheer."

I called my husband. He was working out of the city in

those years. I told him everything, and we commiserated with each other, but I noticed that, while I was telling my husband all this, a voice was also talking to me. "It is not the time to panic for the boy. Be relaxed. It will be good." I told my husband to be calm. I took a break and thought about my son's decision. Maybe he needed more time. But he explained he wasn't thinking he needed more time because he had already begun researching medical schools on the internet, and through several education offices. It was the first week of his searching. He was looking for medical schools in England and Germany. Meanwhile, I learned by chance that Charles University Faculty of Medicine in Prague, the Czech Republic will accept international students, and it was to hold a special examination in two and half months from that point. My son was excited, and my heart started to pound as soon as I got this information.

I had been interested in spirituality for years. I was aware of the importance of signs in life. This timing excited both of us.

He immediately started correspondence, registered for the exam, and demonstrated his strength in the next two and a half months. He was working hard, and I was praying for the highest good for him. So, he was accepted for the exam, and we all bought our flight tickets, booked a nice hotel to support his chances, and arrived in Prague.

What a feeling! I felt like we were all ready to take the exam.

During out first night in Prague, I was meditating after my son and husband fell asleep. I prayed to God, and connected to angels. I was deep in meditation when I saw a cloudy space, which was different from previous ones. There was a strange uncertainty. I could have waited quietly in that space, but I was inpatient. I wanted to move quickly by greeting the unknown and asking directly: "Will my son be successful in his exam?" Immediately, the faces of two beings appeared. They were unlike any beings I had seen before. They were rust-colored, as if made of iron. The one behind didn't speak at all, but the face in front moved a little closer to me and showed itself. He was imposing; he wore a high helmet or a crown on his head. After he looked at me harshly, he said "Yes, he will pass the exam." And then he disappeared. I was thankful for the answer, but I was startled. I could not understand what kind of beings they were. He acted as if he was disturbed. I couldn't sleep comfortably that night with dozens of questions in my mind.

The next day we all went to the exam venue. My son was trying to stay calm. It was a long exam consisting of several parts.

While he was taking the exam, my husband and I visited the famous Czech composer's Antonín Dvořák Museum, which is located on a side street. Beautiful music was playing all over the museum, the fragrant roses in the garden were divine, and all the memories of Dvořák were impressive. I was in another realm. I was feeling angelic presence, and grateful while sitting in the rose garden under the midday sun. It was towards two o'clock, that we went back to the exam building, and the winners list was already posted on the hallway's wall. Hundreds of exhibitors from all over the world were here. I saw my son walking calmly a little further but as soon as I saw his face I understood something was wrong.

"My name is not on the list; I did not win," he said coldly. Although he did not show it, he was sad.

What? This could not be possible!

Two hours ago, between two exam sessions, my son had said clearly his exam was going well.

I just froze in the school hallway. My husband said, "Don't be sad son, God's opportunities never end." He was upset. I could not believe this. How could the story end like this? Those iron-faced men had come to me; they answered me. I didn't know who they were, but I just knew that what I've lived in meditation never could be a lie. I walked sadly out of the school building. My husband was more calm.

I was confused. With every step I took, a wave of disapproval and objection was rising in me. We walked through the old town. I didn't know why I did this, but I walked along the Vltava River aimlessly, with my husband and son following along silently. I was walking with many feelings and doubts in me. Even I was wondering if there were injustices in the exam.

My son called "Mom, where are you taking us? You don't even know anything about here!"

I said, "I don't know, but it might be good to walk for a bit."

We came to the tourist area, and the streets were crowded. I've always heard the name of Charles Bridge. We were very close to the bridge. But the road was blocked after fifty meters. It was full of crowds leaving a nearby stadium where a game had just ended. None of us expected this mess, an incredible noise, nobody could walk. I just saw my son and husband moving quickly towards the bridge. I was stuck in the middle of the crowd. Seeing that the road was fully blocked by people, I waited at the same point. I don't know exactly how it happened, as if a force pushed me in the opposite direction of the Bridge and suddenly turned me to the right side. There was an enormous statue in front of me, it was metal. I looked at the top of the four figures and immediately recognized him.

He was looking around with that same greatness; he was holding a historical foundation certificate and the seal of Charles University in his hand. He was the King, the founder of the University in 1300's, with the same gaze, same iron and bronze face, just like in my vision. When I looked at his face, I was filled with anger.

"Are you happy now? He did not win. Are you pleased by the outcome?"

Oh, my God, I was talking to a statue! I was sad because I believed my son deserved to win. I was angry with myself. Sobs were shaking my whole body; I cried quietly. All people on the road were happy; I was hearing laughter from all sides. I was drunk with this pressure. I felt helpless. The crowd was constantly hitting me.

I suddenly heard a loud noise. I thought it was a gun blast which was strong enough to drown out all other noise. Then it transformed into a voice and spoke to me instantly.

"What are you doing here? It's done. Go, go right now!"

The voice was so strong that I felt like fainting. I tried to look around, everyone was trying to go towards the bridge, and nobody seemed to have heard that voice. At that time, I saw my husband coming back to look for me. As soon as he saw my face, he said   "Oh my goodness! Are you okay?"

"We have to go back right away; please don't ask me anything," I said and added, "Please let's go back to the school immediately. Something happened and must be fixed."

My son came a little later too; I could not explain anything. I could never hurt my son. His father barely persuaded him, and we quickly got back to the school.

I believed I had received divine guidance to alert me to a possible mistake. Hours had passed already. There was nobody at the facility. My son spoke to an officer telling him that we wanted to talk to the faculty examination board chairman. The officer said that this was impossible and that the exam results had been finalized.

My son, who had been silent until now said, "Mom, my sadness has increased fifty times now. Don't you see? I could not win."

I was feeling awful. I made him more upset because of my ego. I spoke with a statue; I heard a special voice in the middle of thousands of people. It was just crazy.

We were walking as three speechless and heartbroken people. When I walked into the central train station's garden, the nightingales were chirping with joy. Several students were studying on benches; lovers were walking hand in hand. The opera house opened doors in all its glory. I tried to tidy myself up until I came to the hotel. I was sad but I was trusting God and angels.

As we approached the hotel, I felt surrender and acceptance of all of us, as if something refreshed our hearts. We came to our rooms, my son wanted to check his emails on the computer. I was just seated when he suddenly screamed, "I won! Mom! I won! "

He started running with the computer while also reading

to us. This was an apology email. It had been sent to us hours ago. An error had been made when the winners' name list was organized. His exam was so successful that, after this mistake, they did not even invite him to the oral exam and added that they would accept his final registration the next day.

It's hard to explain our feelings that evening. We had experienced the miracle. I was in heaven. I expressed my eternal gratitude to angels.

The next day, my husband and son went to the faculty together to enroll, but I decided to go back to the bridge to get answers. I left the hotel early in the morning to go to the bridge. I was fidgety. It was so quiet, I couldn't believe it. It felt as if yesterday's apocalyptic crowd had never happened. I paused for a moment when I came to King Charles' statue. I just stood there and thanked him for establishing Europe's oldest medical school in the 1300's.

I couldn't stay there any longer because I was thinking about the voice I'd heard yesterday, about that amazing energy flowing towards me from the bridge. There was a divine beauty in the air. I was very excited. I felt like I had an invitation from the divine realm. That's exactly what I felt.

I passed under the bridge tower and started walking on the bridge; it was decorated with sculptures on both sides. When I stepped onto the bridge, I felt something pulling me forward softly. When I'd been taken by this energy to the middle of the bridge, an angelic voice was telling me, "You could walk a little more."

I suddenly saw a light shining from the sky to a statue. Every step I took was like a flutter in my heart. Now, an invisible but magnificent energy surrounded me that I wanted to both laugh and cry. The two most magnificent angel statues that I've ever seen in my life were in front of me. There has never been an angel statue in my life that has affected me as these did. It was love at first sight. One angel was holding an angelic book; the other angel's flag seemed to be from higher worlds. I tried to understand the text on the marble; the letters were Latin and faded. *"Seraphicus ...their command."*

It was the Seraph who called out to me on that exam day. He warned me to go back so that I would not be sorry in vain. When he did call me back, he was referring to the hotel, not the university. If we had gone to the hotel instead of the school, we would have been able to get the e-mail sent to my son immediately.

I couldn't understand this call correctly; it was a good idea to ask him where I should go. But whatever happened, by going there I understood the vision's meaning in my meditation.

I visited the statues of the Seraphim for seven years every time I went to Prague.

The Seraph had brought his first signs into my life years ago and in a different way; now his light is my guide on my spiritual path.

Dilek Bayezid became a Seraphim Blueprint teacher in 2013. She teaches these unique energies passionately, and enjoys doing sessions as a spiritual coach. She is nature lover; living on Antalya's shores, and Istanbul by sharing Seraphim Blueprint's light to enable us to realize ourselves.

Angel Action

Dark angels, white angels—the ebony of night beckons the
solstice of day.
I drift this planet in the Singapore of Springtime—flowers
capture my essence;
I am a body in blur of motion—I both salute and sing for
my food
and speak unknown sonnets into the wind.

Garments lie and rest—hangered in my closet of
thoughts—apparel,
on the other hand, is the sparrow I hold inside my hand—
flying in stillness.
Wings sometimes can be wigs—I am captured on a stage,
so many saints and unknown faces in this vast audience.

I deliver lines—sometimes sharp and defined, holding
an edge.
Sometimes a white tunic signs me up for voice lessons—
turtles soon doves.
Oh, how I love to sing—a choir of high notes requires—a
good sleepwalking tenor.
I roam the mountain tops of heavens as I read more about
fairy tales.

Sometimes I live in a forest—there are visitors that walk out
of trees.
I am laughter—I am lost—I am long and lonely—I am
veiled in sobriquet.
How many angels can fit into the color spectrum of slender
imagination?
There is an old unshaved-wood stove parked right in the
middle of my cabin.

There are windows—sparse but affording a Seraphim view.
Archangel window glass is so thin, tensile and transparent—I am at one
with the thick underbrush of direction that is directionless
all around me.
What is it—that has brought my spirit into this Parisian
avenue of earth?

Will I ever be able to soar with a morning robin—making
the rounds
pulling up delectable worms tilling through the soil of
pre-dawn magic.
It is the lightness of the rising sun—a path of angel dust—
that summons
my eyes to release the optical sovereignty that follows me
like—shadow.

John Berns is a man forked in the road of existence—angel
wing heart opening to his left (the feminine side)—narra-
tives, explanations and linear eye sites to the right. Leaving
the 'fracture' of time, he journeys deep within the circumfer-
ence of humanity. He lives in San Francisco, by the ocean—
and the ocean lives (in sanctuary) by him.

Angels Abound

As a child, I loved reading stories of angels; and, as a teenager, I immersed myself in watching Christmas stories where angels were present. I collected angel figurines and read every book I could find about angel interventions. Becoming an adult, I began seeing angels and experiencing the support of angels. Eventually, I began to commune with angels for my highest good and for that of others.

Over the years, I have learned that there are at least one hundred angels behind every Guardian Angel, and each angel is just waiting for a job from us. However, in our human form we forget to ask our angels for guidance or even for basic daily support. Today, I see the angels around my clients and often hear their messages of encouragement and comfort. In our Community Healing Session, there are always angels in the room attending to our guests, some with wings and others in street clothing.   Angels   are walking with us in our daily lives as our friends, family and mentors. Often, angels are here in human form growing spiritually themselves. During a human incarnation, many angels forget where they came from. Several angels offered to be here to give compassion and enlightenment to those spiritual beings having a human experience. And, angels are working through us as we allow our channels of Love and Light to be used to support ourselves and others. Yes, angels abound everywhere. I recall when meeting a client for the first time and seeing their tiny white angel wings. It was such a surprise to witness this. Over the months and years of energy healing therapy and spiritual growth, the client's wings were growing larger. As my client unloaded the dramas and traumas of her life on the earth plane and turned inward to find her true Source of all Love and Light, she began to accomplish her purpose of learning to be love, giving only love, allowing only love into and for her being. This person was here from the angelic realms to grow spiritually, to learn compassion, kindness, forgiveness and lessons of love. This beautiful being had gotten a little off track in their very human form, and now she was moving forward rapidly with her spiritual development plan.

Another amazing experience was when I attended a prayer session at a local church. I was greatly moved when witnessing a huge male angelic being playing the crystal bowls through the human musician. The angel's wings were golden, intricately woven in a geometric pattern and reached from the floor, almost to the ceiling of the church. As the musician moved from crystal bowl to crystal bowl across the platform, repeatedly, the angel moved with him. I closed my eyes to refocus, thinking that I was perhaps imagining this. When I opened my eyes, the angel remained over the musician and played heart-opening music for over an hour. I was in awe.

It was a blessing when I met George. As was our habit when driving anywhere, my husband had popped open the trunk of his car so I could put my rather large pocketbook in, hoping to be more comfortable in the movie theater. This was a rainy night, so we were hustling through the parking lot to get to the theater. Suddenly, I heard a very distinct male voice say, "Go back and get your pocketbook out of the car". As I continued forward without taking action, I saw George. George presented as a young sandy-haired man dressed in a red, green, and beige- plaid, long-sleeved shirt. He came in over my left shoulder, and strongly repeated, "Go back and get your pocketbook out of the car". This time, I listened. I quickly told my husband that we needed to go back to the car for my pocketbook. Well, my husband was not at all happy as we ran back to the car through the misty rain. I got a lecture all the way. But, we went back and got my pocketbook out of the trunk.

When we came out of the movie theater a few hours later, my husband's car was gone. I was so grateful to George for coming to my rescue. My husband was again not happy because his favored golf clubs were in the trunk of the car. It was only after the incident that I had the courage to tell my husband the story of George's visit.

This next encounter was one of faith. I had been co-hosting a Community Healing Session for eight years. One evening, something made me pull out my phone and quickly take two photos. Later that night when I looked at the photos, I saw the most amazing cherubs. Yes, two cherubs, one dressed in light blue with white wings, and the other all in white. In each photo a cherub was sitting in the lap of a specific guest. I knew the woman was active in our church, but I did not know the woman, or any of her life stories. When I called to tell her what was captured in the photo, she became emotional. This lovely woman had had several miscarriages, but she still felt close to two of the fetuses. She had come to the Community Healing Session for this very reason, to perhaps connect with the babies. And so it was that night, that her personal wishes were fulfilled. Thank you, Creator!

As a Guide to the House of Saint Ignatius of Loyola in Abadiania, Brazil, I often see angels and energy there and catch them on film. There is one "Entity of Light", as the spirit healers are called that are seen all the time. I see this "Entity of Light" in the daylight and in the evening sky. It is a huge expansive pink energy. Some think perhaps this is Archangel Chamuel; others say it is Jesus. The energy is so large, it fills a court yard and spreads over the top of a building. The essence is pure love.

Always, when I can't sleep and have prayed for everyone I can think of, I'll call in my angels to bring the sleeping dust. Once, as I was saying the request for the angels to bring in the sleeping dust, I immediately saw a female angel. She had long wavy blond hair and was floor to ceiling in height. Her sparkling sky blue and yellow dress touched the floor, and her wings filled the entire wall left to right. She took my breath away. I was asleep in a second.

During private energy healing sessions, I call in the guardian angels of my clients. Some come in ancient garb; others show as radiant light; some are dressed in street clothing or tunics, and clothing of various periods in time. Angels of all sizes, with and without wings, dressed in every color of the rainbow come for the clients. It is so humbling to witness their presence and watch them go to work releasing their charges from worries, sadness, pain, blame, shame, and all sorts of past life, lifelong and every day traumas. Remember, angels abound, and we only need to call them in.

Angels, fairies, and other healers in spirit are often working within the chakras, our energy system. They also work within the subtle or invisible bodies of our auric field, releasing negative energies, psychic attacks, fears and emotional blocks, which we have held onto for days, years, and, at times, most of a lifetime or over many life times. As the healers work with humans, they are freeing the stuck energy, and these blocks or negative energies move to the Light. Their work leaves us in a state of peacefulness, feeling lighter and freer.

As messengers of our Creator of All That Is (God, Source, The Divine, Our Beloved, The One, I AM, Jesus, Buddha, Universal Life Force Energy, Light), angels often push us ever so gently. They give us creative insights, longings, hunches, and inspiration. In dreams, they bring past, present, and future wisdom. Angels have all kinds of abilities, jobs and duties as they assist us in our earthly purposes. Our job is to call them in and ask for their help, assistance, support, and guidance. We are not meant to walk this lifetime alone. However, we have free will. Ask and you are surely heard. Ask again. And, ask some more. Always give gratitude ahead of time, and see the fulfillment of your request.

I remember feeling stuck and thinking that I should return to my prior corporate work of 80 hours a week of troubleshooting, re-engineering business practices, and tons of stress. But the work was exciting and challenging. I connected with a group of fifty women from all over the world, who were taking a ten-week course on writing and publishing. During the class, we would participate in two sessions with a psychic. The organizer asked each of us to send in five questions, some of which would be answered by the psychic during our class.

Okay, so I was excited. I sent in five personal questions, never truly considering that out of 250 questions, mine would be on a global scale, questions relating to world peace and Earth healing. The questions were far from personal considerations. Well, during the first week, the psychic was answering questions from our group. I was holding my breath, hoping that my personal questions were not addressed during this two-hour call.

As the next week approached, I considered not even dialing into the class. My anxiety was building. Heaven forbid the psychic should pull a personal question to respond to. But, after much debate with myself, I did dial into the call. The psychic pulled the fifth question of the night, and I held my breath as the psychic read one of my questions out loud to the group.

I was sitting in my den with one large candle lit on the table in front of me, my water, pen and notebook beside me. Suddenly, I noticed a large golden yellow, almost orange light behind me. This light was filling the space on the entire wall. As the psychic was answering my question, the light grew larger and brighter. I could feel the light all around me until I was totally engulfed in this brilliant light. My heart was wide open as the sweat was building around my temples, forehead and neck. The psychic's channeled response continued for what seemed like a long time.

When she was done, a participant on the phone asked the psychic whom she was channeling. Another asked whose question it was. Again, I was holding my breath hoping the psychic would not divulge that the question was mine. The psychic answered that Archangel Uriel had been the angel who responded to the question. She mentioned that the Archangel Uriel's colors are golden, yellow and orange light. She continued, saying that Uriel offers his support in business and growth. Of course, the host of the class emailed the recording of the message to me, and I have listened to it repeatedly, feeling Archangel Uriel's support and guidance throughout my whole being. What a gift! I feel the need to share this message because others, like me have the same or similar question.

This was my question: "What is it that I can do to continue to make a difference? My past career was wonderful, but I feel lost right now, lost in trying to determine what my work should be now."

The Archangel Uriel answered, "Take away the word *should*. You are experiencing growth. You are now ready to take a step forward, and you are clinging to the old. This is a natural process. Once you have done all that you need to do, there will be a new doorway for which you are becoming ready. This is the space between where you were and where you are going. This space feels uncomfortable for you. You must decide what you wish to create, not what you *should* create. You are in charge of your life and where it will go. You are in charge. Take this time now to search within, to connect with your guardian angel and your guides, so that your heart may be open to possibilities.

"And pay attention because we are speaking to you. We are giving you signs. We are giving you ideas. But, because this is not what you have always done, you feel you are making this up. You are making new choices based on our guidance.

We are always here. We are always ready to pull you forward or push you if necessary, but we can only take you forward if you agree. Allow yourself quiet time to connect to your spirit. Pay attention to what comes to you, what you hear from others, what you are attracted to, and what you see around you.

"Dear One, what attracts you, now? Do not abandon what you have done if it still helps others. What you did before was good. Make your new decisions based on what you truly wish to create. That is the hard part. When you decide, we are here, and when you are ready we will make it happen faster than you can believe. But, do not rush it and do not struggle to find it. Open! Open yourself to possibilities and do not be afraid. This is *your* life. You are here to enjoy and to be joyful.

"When one activity that brings you joy has to come an end, it is up to *you* to choose what to replace it with. See what is in front of you. Enjoy quiet time. Sink into it. Release all doubts. Release all fears. Just be, and you will hear us. You will receive your messages from us. What you create again will be as joyful and as rewarding and as blessed as any work you have done before. Now, you are at a new place, a place where you deliberately connect to the Higher-Self, to the All that Is.

"There are many now on your planet that are moving forward to bring more people to a place of understanding of their spiritual nature. If you are willing, you will continue to be a blessing to others. Do not be afraid of this place. It feels like you are lost, but you are not. You are surrounded by possibilities and potential. If you can accept this with expectation and joyful patience, it will come forth. And you will be a blessing to others and joyful in your being.

"Now, to figure out if you are guided or if it is your ego? How do we know? Guidance never comes from frustration. Guidance is always uplifting. When you are blocked from moving forward, you are not following guidance. Everything flows when you are following guidance. Turn it over to your guides and angels. Give them the anxiety. Give them the frustration. Be open and listen. Surrender and release. Use your spiritual practice."

Wow! By now, I was in a full-on sweat, soaked from head to toe. And the Light behind me was still radiating brilliant yellow, orange and white. I had to remind myself to just breathe.

I am learning that God speaks to us in many ways. If we can get silent and go within, we can begin to co-create our lives with the Creator. The messengers and support will be there. We will be guided, always, if we surrender and allow. As we truly intend to open our hearts to receive through various venues such as dreams, encounters with strangers and with friends, or through meditation and prayer, our questions will be answered.

Guides come for a time, or for a project, a soul relation-ship, a career, or perhaps for an entire season in our lives. A long time ago, I met a beautiful guide. At the time, I thought of her as a goddess. Years later, when taking Seraphim Level III, I heard her identify herself as a Seraph. She did not have wings, which confused my human mind. However, she brought me through a very difficult time, a time I could relate to now as a crucifixion and resurrection period. A part of me was dying from the pain and trauma of my life, but with her help, my higher self could pull me forward.

She presents as a beautiful Hawaiian woman, somewhat like what I imagine a goddess would look like. She is young, appearing in her early 30's and full of life force energy. Our journey together began by visiting several of my past lives. Initially, these were multiple lives spent with one particular soul, my first husband in this lifetime. The guide took me through time, showing me various venues where I witnessed enough pain, trauma and sorrow to gain the courage to act. In several of the journeys, there was another key soulmate. Together, the two soulmates and I were creating a three-soul love triangle. This love triangle was playing out again in my current life. Seeing this repeatedly in multiple past lives and feeling the emotions, allowed me to finally release, forgive, and let go of both individuals. I was done with the lessons and with both soulmates. I was now free to move forward in this lifetime, allowing myself more joy, peace, and self-love. And I could allow myself to be loved fully and completely.

The journey into my past lives was so visual, so real, I just knew with every part of my being it was my soul's truth. Today, I can remember every detail of the past-life regression class, even though it happened over 35 years ago.

This angelic guide's presence in my current life continued for many more years, all the remaining years I'd spent in my corporate career path. She appeared in dreams, showing me situations beyond repair along with opportunities. Some of the opportunities I would spearhead, and others she would be leading through me. All I needed to do was to open my heart, listen to my intuition, and allow my channel to be used.

During this time, I was asking for direction, as well as for support, in my daily career life. Much joy, peace, and harmony was accomplished as my angelic guide and I worked together for the greater good of thousands of lives. Money was made for the corporations who hired me, but it was always a four-way win, a win for the employees, the providers, the membership, as well as the corporations.

As I look back, I opened myself as a channel of Love and Light, always asking *Creator of All That Is* to use me. Use me God as a vessel, a vessel to heal, to build, to resolve, to enlighten others. I am here, God, use me now. Yes, angels abound. Ask for their guidance. Ask more. Ask again. Live in a state of gratitude.

Karen Coratelli-Smith is a Spiritual Counselor, Energy Healing Practitioner, Past Life Regression Counselor, Shaman Mesa Carrier, Esoteric Healer, Cranio-Sacral Therapist, Seraphim Blueprint practitioner, and Theta Healing Instructor.

My Four-legged Guru

There he was lying in my arms. His breathing was slowing down. I didn't know what to do, feel or think other than staring at him. He was so calm. He took a deep breath, released it and was gone. At that instant, a part of me went with him, leaving a painful empty hole in my heart. A dull, grievous silence took that empty space in me and started to expand. It would have taken over my whole being if I had not witnessed how gracefully and trustfully he had surrendered into the divine void. So, I hugged him and gave him a last kiss. My mind was telling me that he was just a dog, but my heart knew that he was so much more. A special soul who inspired me in so many ways over the past ten years.

When Brandy came into my life I was lost—lost in my overcrowded and hyperactive mind, lost in a fast moving, harshly-behaving world. Everything felt superficial and disposable, but that didn't prevent me from wanting more. I couldn't resist the urge to consume. I thought that this was the only way to exist, to be someone. Getting a dog was also just adding another possession to my life.

So, I bought him as I would buy a new designer handbag, or a piece of jewelry. I wanted to show him off, add value to who I am. Surely, it had to be a King Charles Cavalier—bred exclusively for royals. But soon, a harsh reality crashed my dreams. I found out that a dog is not an accessory. It is a living being with its own character, flaws, and spirit.

The first couple weeks, I spent hours on the internet searching for the most effective ways to train him, and, the rest of the day, I would apply all these techniques on Brandy, hoping that he soon would turn into the perfect dog. But no matter how hard I tried, he was always disobedient and stubborn, and he even had the doggedness to bite me occasionally. The more I insisted on rules and limitations, the harsher his responses became. It turned into a desperate struggle between us with no progress at all. One day, I reached my breaking point. I cannot forget how I dropped down on the floor in front of my five-month old puppy, disappointed, crying, and feeling totally hopeless.

Then the unexpected happened. The barking, peeing and biting little monster dropped the toy he was tearing into pieces, jumped on my lap and looked at me with his big brown eyes. I felt that, through these eyes, he was pouring love into me. That flow of unexpected compassion gave my heart a jump start, and that moment marked the beginning of a wonderful journey.

We never did another training session again. Instead, I started to observe him. After a while, I realized that he was just trying to grow and learn how to survive in the harsh environment I was imposing upon him.

Soon, I started to understand that he was mirroring me, and reflecting all my flaws back to me. He showed me that my attempts to control everything in my life were the main reason why I was so tense and unhappy. It was not his behavior that was driving me mad; it was me, working against myself, unbalanced, unconscious, and enslaved by my mind, I was living a life inharmonious with my soul. He showed me that the person I was representing in my current life had little resemblance with who I truly was.

Now that I had discovered this, I needed to connect with my true self, and I started to search for spiritual workshops. And just a couple days later, I came upon a healing system that intrigued me at first glance. A fresh start with a new modality was just what I was looking for. I signed up for a class right away. The very first time I was initiated into these amazing energies, I felt that I was on the right path and that my life would change accordingly.

This amazing new healing system was called "Seraphim Blueprint", and it had eleven universal energies put together in six levels by the Seraphic consciousness. It took me almost one year to complete all of them.

With every new level of the Seraphim Blueprint, I felt more liberated. The more I connected with Seraphim Consciousness, the more my mind relaxed. My hyperactive thoughts lost their pulling powers. All the painful emotions that made me cling to the past healed one after the other, and I became more able to stay in the moment.

After a while, something wonderful happened. I started to meditate. I loved it. When I closed my eyes, I opened to stillness. In this magical stillness, all my thoughts and worries disappeared, and I could go deep into my heart. There, I saw a divine spark that connected me with Divine consciousness, and the more I opened my heart, the more Divine love poured into me. I felt that my whole body was filled with joyful calmness. I began to expand, until I was one with all there is. Then I heard my breath, and, following this rhythmic tune of life, I found my way back to my heart. And there it was. Embedded in my heart in the core of my body, sparkling in so many colors, I found the secret of life: Hope. It was an amazing, blissful experience.

But as soon as I opened my eyes, my mind took charge, belittling my experience and telling me to focus on all the real issues of life. But then again, there had been a shift in me. I had the feeling that what I perceived as reality was tainted by my feelings, experiences and expectations. Captured by this illusion, I made choices that made me unhappy because they were not in tune with my true self.

So, I continued to meditate; I loved to go deep inside my heart and connect with the Divine spark that was more in tune with me than my self-centered mind. When I closed my eyes, I attuned to myself, and that made me balanced and happy. When I opened my eyes, my mind took over, and that made me worried and unhappy. But I couldn't live my life with my eyes closed. So, how could I transfer this elevating state of divine bliss into the world I was living in?

I stepped out in the garden. Brandy was lying there enjoying the sun and doing nothing else. He was relaxed and carefree. Didn't he live in the same world as I did? How could he be so happy? He looked at me with his wise eyes, and his soothing energy made me forget my worries. Then I looked around me: the birds were chirping joyfully, the flowers radiated cheerfulness. My bossy mind full of thoughts, of daily haggle and struggle seemed to have lost its power and surrendered into this peaceful, yet vibrant presence that embraced me as my garden. I could swear I saw a smile on Brandy's face when he came towards me. Or was that a re- flection of the big smile I had on my own face? He started to lick my hand as if he wanted to tell me that this state of bliss is so powerful because it is a collective consciousness. All that appeared since my garden was composed of many, many tiny parts united together, vibrating harmoniously in the same blissful frequency that created this uplifting presence. Together, they formed a united consciousness that overpowered my disruptive individual mind. Brandy hopped on my lap as if he was confirming my intuitive thoughts.

Maybe I needed to find the Divine spark in my heart on my own, but once I made that connection I needed to open and share hope and love with others. That way, my joyful heart could become a part of a joyful presence that consisted of many, many joyful hearts, and, together, we could create a joyful reality. If plants and animals could do it, we humans must be able to do this as well. The excitement that filled my body was almost intoxicating. I understood how powerful we are in creating our reality and that we become even more powerful when we unite.

But these illuminating feelings didn't last long. As soon as I stepped out of the garden to take a walk with Brandy, I found myself among unhappy, rude and stressed-out people. My mind took charge once more and ridiculed all my intentions to spread joy and love into the world. But I knew that I wasn't my mind anymore. I had managed to escape the daunting cage of my mind and had become aware of new perspectives. It was a huge transformation for me, and since the Seraphim Blueprint energies played an important part in it, I decided to become a teacher of this amazing spiritual system.

I believe that all humans and their individual minds are connected and that, together, they form the collective human consciousness which creates, or at least affects the reality we live in. So, if I could share the Seraphim energies with others, maybe they would also be inspired to connect with the Divine spark in their hearts and start radiating hope. The more people would radiate hope, the more potent this Divine gift would become, and this could create a healthy base for universal love to grow. And love is the ultimate energy to create a better world, don't you agree?

So, I decided to become a Seraphim Blueprint teacher and took teacher-training for all six levels, trusting that the universe would give me all the support I needed. But although I was ready to teach right away, I didn't know how to attract students. So, I contacted spiritual centers to find out if I could teach the Seraphim Blueprint energies at their premises, but since this system was new, they weren't familiar with it and declined right away. I was disappointed. I felt like I was experiencing the same restricting effects that I had initially experienced with my bounded mind. Only this time, I had encountered a collective resistance.

One day, I was sitting in my garden, charging myself with the beautiful energies that surrounded me. Brandy was sleeping beside me. Sparrows were chirping joyfully and taking funny leaps into the air like kids playing in a pool. The trees were chatting to each other with every breeze that came through. Every breath I was taking in this presence was uplifting and filled me with love and gratitude. Once more, I wished with all my heart to find a way to share this blissful state with as many people as possible. I was just about to meditate with my favorite Seraphim Blueprint energies when Brandy woke up. A butterfly with beautifully colored wings was flying around us and performing a graceful dance. Soon another one joined, and when Brandy tried to catch them, they accelerated their intricate movements even more, and Brandy became a part of their performance. I couldn't resist grabbing my phone and taking a video. I felt that sharing this random, but, at the same time, very special moment, could uplift others as well. Suddenly, it occurred to me that I could also make a video about the Seraphim Blueprint energies to share my heartfelt enthusiasm with others. As if he read my mind, Brandy turned away from the dancing butterflies and hopped on the garden chair I was sitting in. His big brown eyes said, "Let's do it".

That was the day I made an introductory video explaining the six Seraphim Blueprint levels—of course, with Brandy just beside me. I shared it on social media. Soon, I found myself using this lively and effective virtual network more often. This opened a whole new world for me. A world that overrode the borders and limitations of distance and time, thus forming communities and gathering around mutual goals and beliefs became so much easier. I started to teach the Seraphim Blueprint energies online. After a while, I had my own group of students, and we were doing powerful meditations together. I was thrilled to experience a bond with people I had never met in person. Witnessing how they transformed into more balanced and content versions of themselves motivated me to teach more.

My initial small group of Seraphim Blueprint students got bigger, and the more we communicated, shared experiences, and did group meditations, the more joy we were spreading. This joy expanded even more when we joined other Seraphim Blueprint groups. Now, when we come together for online events, we have a group with participants from many different countries. Although we don't speak the same language and live miles away from each other, we unite with love and hope in our hearts.

Today, I feel blessed to be able to share all the gifts and experiences that the Seraphim consciousness opened for me. I feel myself useful, fulfilled and alive. I wake up to embrace every new day with excitement. Brandy, with his unconditional love and devotion, was my companion and inspiration from the beginning and my guide and protector until his last day. Maybe he passed on because his work with me was done. Maybe he wanted me to learn that being present when a person close to you passes is an inspiring moment. Maybe he wanted me to remember my emotions and write this story.

Maybe he wanted me to know that if we breathe, and our heart is beating, we are a part of human consciousness. We are powerful, and we can create a world full of hope and love—a world where we can manifest our best selves.

Inspired by the beauty and power of Seraphim Blueprint energies, **Özden Öke** became a Seraphim Blueprint Teacher in 2013. Soon afterwards, she started to do soul readings and healing sessions. She has become Turkey's Seraphim Blueprint National Leader and is organizing and translating spiritual workshops for Seraphim Blueprint and other modalities in Turkey.

Lessons from a Baby Angel

Watching the sky on a clear starry night are Mimi and her grandson, Luke. Even though Luke would never tell his friends, he really does enjoy his "talking" time with his grandmother. On this night, they are watching the stars in the night sky, when they witness a shooting star, and his grandmother, says, "Ahhh, a special angel is born tonight." He had never heard her say this and asked her what she meant. She reminded him of the time she told him about the Great Divine Mother, and how she sits with you just before birth and helps you pick out your own star. Yes, he remembered. Well, the shooting stars are special baby angels being born, who will have a path of one day becoming an Earth angel. It is very special.

Luke says, "Tell me." Mimi smiles and says, "Okay, it is time for you to know. Divine Mimi Mother works with Divine Father in watching over the whole world and universe. When the stars are ready, they are chosen for all kinds of 'jobs' and go to Heaven for schooling. There, more learning is centered on how they can help mankind. Some train to help with depression, sadness, and small children. Others have happier jobs like helping new babies learn basic skills, helping people with happiness, joy, and success. But occasionally, a baby star angel arrives, and everyone in heaven rejoices because they know that this baby angel has agreed to go to Earth to be a soul for a human who is destined to make a difference in the world and will need guidance.

"On this night, you have witnessed such a birth of a baby angel," and adds, "Do you want to hear about a baby star angel that I have known"?

"Oh yes", says Luke, "tell me everything".

"This new angel was so sweet with little baby wings that can hardly fly yet. She has so much sparkle about her, she almost leaves glitter footprints. She has many lessons to learn, and heaven is rejoicing at her arrival. First, she is shown around and introduced to everyone. She tells everyone to call her Chrissy. Everyone knew she was different since baby angels do not choose their own names. What a handful she will be! Upon being shown the 'closet of angel wings', she wanted to change out of her baby wings. She was told, 'No, you must earn them, along with the halos'. You can almost see her pouting and stamping her foot. She was like no other baby star ever born, and she had a lot of questions.

"Chrissy learned quickly and kept asking for new wings so that she could fly farther. Again, she was told, not yet. She practiced flying every day and did her best to be helpful and kind. She earned a flight with a master teacher angel to watch over a meditation group that had come together to pray for world peace. She was told to stay within the light folds of the master angel and only observe, being careful not to be seen. All went well until, in her excitement, she stepped out from the master angel energy field, and an intuitive person in the meditation group saw her peeking out. Chrissy got reprimanded, and they left quickly.

"Back to heaven's classroom she was sent to go over the rules again. She learned how to become a butterfly, a dragonfly, and even an orb of light to help her get ready for lessons while traveling to Earth.

"She earned the respect of the master teacher angel and was given another opportunity for more flights from heaven. The ones she enjoyed most were helping children. With excitement, each night as the sun set, she would gather with the older angels in kind of Call Center, waiting and listening for the prayers of young children or a cry out because they were afraid to be in the dark. On these call trips, she lay down with the babies until they fell asleep, or she would hold the hand of a little one who was crying from a nightmare. She did this so well, she was able to go to the closet of wings and choose the next pair. Chrissy was so happy and excited because she knew one day she would complete her schooling and graduate with beautiful wings and a halo.

"Chrissy, sometimes worried that she would not pass her assignments and would be held back from Divine Mother's and Father's plans for her. She worked hard in angel school, and she was given one last challenge to graduate. It was a full moon. She could feel the different energy in the Call Center as she arrived with the other angels. She was given the task of comforting a child who had lost its parents, then a child who had lost a sibling, and lastly, a child who had lost a pet. It is a big responsibility to watch over children all over the world. Chrissy was overwhelmed at first with the sadness of it all, but she knew she had done a great job. Hooray!

"She was given permission to visit the closet of wings and choose the next pair and her first halo. Yes, it was time to leave heaven and spend time on Earth. She ran to the special closet of angel wings. Chrissy got emotional when she saw her baby wings in the back of the closet. She chose the most beautiful new wings in rainbow colors and a silver halo. Chrissy was happy and ready for her new life and journey".

It seemed that Mimi was quiet for a long time, reliving a memory.

Mimi broke the silence and said, "Luke, many people believe that God blesses children with extra care and love. That is why everyone is assigned a guardian angel. And on a rare occasion, an angel is born to become an Earth angel. A special angel who comes to watch over her own children".

But back to the story, "Chrissy flew to Earth with all the other angels wishing her well because they knew, one day, she would always return".

Mimi is quiet again and Luke says, "But what happened to Chrissy? Is she still in heaven or on Earth?"

Mimi smiles and says, "Luke, Chrissy came to Earth, and I named her Christine."

Luke's eyes got big and he started to be overwhelmed with emotions and an inner knowing in his heart.

"Yes, Luke, Chrissy is your mother, Christine."

"What?" Luke whispered, "I knew she was special." Luke gives his grandmother a big hug and jumps up.

Mimi says, "Where are you going, Luke?"

Luke yells back, "I can't wait to tell my sisters, Samantha and Faith. But wait, Mom, Mom, where are you?"

Sandra McGill is a retired certified hypnotherapist, who specializes in meditation and past-life regressions, and has worked with angels for 30 years. She is also a Seraphim Blueprint Teacher, Reiki Master, and Ghost Buster and is trained in Jesus Codes, Theta Healing, Therapeutic Touch, Munay Ki and Ama Deus.

Angels are Real

I did not believe in angels when I met mine. In fact, I had a hissy fit when she came in. She told me something I did not want to hear, so I knew I wasn't imagining it or making it up. I did not thank her for the information, and I wasn't glad to meet her. I say "she" and "her" but angels don't have gender. We perceive them in gender terms, according to the energy they present and the way we sense them.

You may very well ask how I encountered her when I didn't believe she existed in the first place. My partner, the love of my life, made me do it. He'd been telling me for months that he could feel an angelic presence around me, and I'd pooh-poohed the idea.

I was a nice Jewish girl from Queens. What did I know about angels? As far as I was concerned, they were for Goyim along with Santa Claus and the Easter Bunny. I could believe more readily in the tooth fairy.

My first meeting with LNO, for that is her name, is described completely with other transmissions she gave to me in *Ask Your Angels*, a book I wrote with Andrew Ramer. It's a practical hands-on guide that teaches folks how to tune into their celestial helpers. Published in 1992, it's printed in nine languages, and there's even an e-book now. Back in the

90s, pre-email, I received thousands of letters from readers living in all 50 States, Canada, and abroad. Now, almost 30 years later, I hear from second generation readers, who got the book from their mother or found it online. It's a classic, as Andrew and I knew it would become, and it is still being published.

Because of the book, which debuted at the very beginning of the "angel craze," I was invited to do workshops and seminars in New York City, at the Open Center, and upstate at Wainwright House and Omega. I gave talks and did signings at bookshops around the country, combining them with workshops in Portland, Seattle, San Francisco, Denver, Cincinnati, Orlando and Vancouver. Wherever I went, I appeared on local radio and TV shows. I began to be called an angel expert, a description I abominated. Although I wanted to be special, to be admired and, well, all right, venerated, deep down I felt like a phony. Despite extraordinary experiences of angelic interventions, miraculous moments when things happened that could not be rationally explained, insights given that were beyond my ken, I secretly harbored serious doubts. Was I just lucky? Was my angel LNO real? Was I tapping into a goldmine I hadn't earned and didn't deserve? For sure, I was no more an "expert" than anyone else because if, in fact, I was in contact with angels, everyone can communicate with Higher Intelligence. The description "angel expert" smacked of the same separation and elitism I detested in religion, where priests, rabbis, and imams were deferred to because they were said to be closer to God. Nonetheless, vanity prevailed. My ego gladly participated in numerous network TV angel "specials" and enjoyed being recognized afterwards in stores and when traveling.

Even with persistent nagging thoughts that I was making it all up about the angels, they kept coming in and saving the day. As we relate in *Ask Your Angels*, there are different angels for different purposes, ones involved with transportation, gardening, parking, communication, writing books (!), relationships, healing and so on. They want to be of service, to be called upon for the smallest issues to the biggest ones. All you need to do is ask. Buoyed by the success of our book, I travelled extensively throughout the U.S. as well as abroad; I found numerous occasions to call on the angels myself.

In San Francisco, following a publicity and workshop tour, I was driving a rented car on Interstate 280 heading toward the airport. I wanted to stop on my way to buy some special bitter orange-scented incense made by Agraria, a company based there at the time. I had the address on Taylor Street but I was unfamiliar with the area and had no idea which exit I should take to get near it. In those days cars were not equipped with GPS, I had to rely on another source of guidance. I asked the angels to steer me to the correct exit, turning off when I felt prompted. Although the name of the exit was not the same as the one I had for the shop, I wound up on the exact street. I even found a legal parking spot.

As a New Yorker, when you find a legal parking space you take it; mindless of the fact that I had no idea how far I had to go on Taylor Street, I started walking up the steepest hill I'd ever encountered. It took less than a block for me to realize I'd never make my flight back to New York if I didn't get a cab. There wasn't one in sight. In fact, there seemed to be very little traffic at all. What to do? I wasn't going to get back in the car and drive up the hill—suppose I couldn't find a parking space there? Then it dawned on me that I needed to ask the angels for a cab. No sooner had I done so when one appeared out of nowhere.

I gave the cab driver the address and instructed him to wait while I ran into the shop, not quite at the top of the hill but almost. I bought a couple of boxes of the special burning sticks and then jumped into the back of the car. The radio was playing, and when I heard the song, I burst into tears: "Calling All Angels". I made the flight with a little time to spare.

Scheduled to do a talk and book signing at a store near the Seattle College campus, I arrived an hour early and went into a Starbucks to have a cup of coffee. This was several years before Starbucks shops proliferated like mushrooms after the rain, and the name became synonymous with java. As I waited for my latte, I idly picked up a copy of the free penny saver newspaper in the stand near the sugar and milk bar. From the Dale Carnegie Course I'd taken 20 years prior, I remembered that it was always good to address local interests when giving a talk, and I thought I might find something relevant to include. Scanning the calendar of events, I discovered, much to my amazement, that I was listed to give a reading of *Ask Your Angels*, with questions and answers afterward, at the Elliott Bay bookstore three hours later. While I'd been in touch with the store prior to my trip and had wanted to include it in my schedule, I'd never received a confirmation from them.

I got to the second event on time and shared the unusual occurrence because it was a perfect demonstration of a way the angels work—by giving us inner prompts that we think we've originated or were our ideas. When I innocently explained that I'd gotten to my previous engagement too early and had gone into Starbucks "looked like a place where

I could get a cup of coffee", the Seattle audience roared with laughter. The Emerald City is where Starbucks was born.

In Denver, I gave a talk and signed books at the Tattered Cover Bookstore. There was a hefty crowd, probably upwards of 60 or 70 people. The questions were numerous and almost predictable, such as, "My deceased grandmother comes to me in dreams. Is she my guardian angel?" The answer is no, angels are not dead people; they have never been human and rarely appear in human form. Grandma can be a protective spirit guide, but she's not an angel.

I was walking up and down the aisle with a handheld microphone during the Q and A, and then a man asked, "If each of us has a guardian angel with us all the time, where was my son's angel when he fell to his death on a climbing expedition?"

I stopped, dead in my tracks, stymied. What on earth could I say to this man? I didn't have a clue. Panicked, I mentally addressed my angel, "LNO, You got me into this; you've got to get me out. Now!"

As I resumed walking, my heart thumping, I wondered how I could console this man. What could I say? Then, words came. They were not my words because I did not have any idea of what the correct response would be. They just came out of my mouth: "You have suffered a grievous loss, a terrible loss. Anyone who suffers such a loss is called to higher service. Because of this experience, you can help others who have also lost children, to bring them the bitter-sweet wisdom that you have gained."

The talk concluded then, and as I was signing books, the man appeared in front of me. He introduced me to his wife. Then he said, "What you spoke about is true. We started a support group for parents who have lost their children. We've been doing this for about a year now."

Subsequent years and innumerable intervention—some minuscule, a few miraculous—have relieved me of my troublesome doubts. What I know for sure is that angels are real, a vital part of the remarkable transformation of consciousness that is taking place on the planet. Most important now is the message that angels always bring, "Fear not. Be not afraid." We need to heed these words and take heart. We need to remember to ask for their guidance and help, and we need to say, "Thank you" when they answer.

Alma Daniel is an internationally-known author, inspirational speaker and spiritual teacher. Alma was trained and ordained as a non-denominational, interfaith minister. She co-authored the book *Ask Your Angels*, which has sold more than half a million copies, and is published in nine languages. She lives in New York City.

An Angelic Dugong

First, I just want you to know, I am not a marine veterinarian. I have no special training in animal care, and I failed science in high school. Then how did I end up where I am today? Well, I believe the answer is the right mix of human free will and angelic assistance. The following relates how I developed a relationship with the Divine, and how I can perform miracles, without much knowledge of the animal world.

The earliest I can remember where my path into the unseen started was in 1999 in Hutt City, New Zealand. It was where my intuition developed, and my psychic abilities blossomed. There was this purple, sparkly store with glittery stars sprinkled on the carpet. I was drawn in, or should I say was pulled in, each afternoon after school. The store owner, 'Annette', introduced me to all sorts of wonderful aspects of New Age Spirituality, from pendulums, crystals, channeling, and reiki. I became remarkably close to Annette and her family. Eventually, I ended up calling her 'Auntie Annette'. I met many extraordinary people. One was a world-renowned Maori shaman, Wai Turoa Morgan, who became one of my first spiritual masters. I graduated second degree Reiki with Annette when I was just seventeen years old. Coming to think of it now, it must have been an angel who dropped my student ID card somewhere on that starry carpet, otherwise I would not have gone back in and had that first long conversation.

It was fun to learn and experience magic and energies. Everything came easy to me; I was told that I am special, and that I am a natural. So, ever since then, I used my intuition to help people and spirits whenever possible. Yes, there were times when I was so attached to the material world, neglected my spirituality, and then my world spun out of control. However, it is important to know that your one Guardian Angel who chose to be with you since birth had never, and will never, leave you, even if a person decides to walk down the darkest path in their life. I was told just now by my team of angels that even my troubled youthful days were meant to be. 'Without going through those experiences, how would you be able to understand the people you were going to help?'

However, if you do choose to grow spiritually and assist other beings, then you would attract more angels to drop by and join your team. I know a lot of people who asked for the name of their angel. In my teenage days, I used to get stuck with asking for names or with what each angel looked like. They can take any shape and form that they please; the same with names. Most of the time, they choose ones that we would be comfortable with. Now, with so many angels in my team and the ones that come and go, I go with the angel who looks after me for a certain something.

I am not naïve. I have gone through trial and error and many tests to learn to trust my unseen colleagues and to know that I am accurate enough when I go and help people. I tried ways of getting there faster. Or where will I get a parking spot today? Since I live in the physical world, the unseen must be able to deliver certain physical results. Otherwise, how would people believe what they perceive as 'the unknown'? By this point, I trust my team fully to the point where, if they told me to jump off a cliff, I would do so.

After I came back to Thailand in 2006, I hopped from one company to another for seven years. During that period, I went through life as a normal person would have. I was brought back into the spiritual side of life in 2014. I read Judy Hall's crystal encyclopedia and really wanted to get a piece of Auralite23. A voice I have not heard for a long time popped out of nowhere and told me to visit a crystal shop in a shopping mall. It was that day that I learnt of Ruth and the Seraphim, and her energy system called 'Seraphim Blueprint'. That evening, I realized that I had strayed from my entire spiritual path and daily practices into living a chaotic, busy modern life. So, I started to converse and catch up with my angels and got back to helping other people by using clairvoyance, clairaudience and channeling.

However, I did not pursue Seraphim Blueprint training until 2018. I finished my training and continued to most of the advanced levels by February 2019. The Seraphim Blueprint became the source for amazing energy tools that I leaned on in all parts of my life, and to which I turned when I wanted to help others. It was with this energy system that I continued to explore and receive so many opportunities to further my abilities to help Gaia and her children. (Note: the energy mentioned from here on will be of the Seraphim Blueprint system, they will be in italics and if you feel that you resonate with them, you can visit www.seraphimblueprint.org for more details.)

By around mid-2019, I started to get fed up with helping people, especially those with stubborn egos and issues of self-identity. It was to the point that when I conversed with the Seraph and my angelic team, I asked if I could move away from working with souls in need, but still be able to do good in the world? The answer I received was, 'The opportunity will come; you should finish up whatever you are currently doing.' So, I began to finish all the cases I was then handling.

In August 2019, my life took a turn in a totally different direction. I received a strong call to volunteer to be a caretaker for stranded, marine mammals. I applied and I got the job, but I had to travel down south from Bangkok to Phuket on Mother's Day. I chose to go.

I was given the opportunity to work with either a baby whale, or a baby dugong. I first volunteered to look after the stranded baby dwarf sperm whale named 'Hope'. I knew of 'Jamil' the dugong baby, but I thought that working with a baby whale would be a rarer opportunity than working with a dugong. I had to choose because they carry different strands of bacteria that cannot be mixed with each other. So, if I touched a whale, I would not be able to touch a dugong right away.

First, I used the Aqua energy of Quantum Hyper Communication to communicate with the Seraphim of the sea, to be accepted by them. After I felt accepted, I kept using the same energy to communicate with the guardian angel of Hope, the baby whale. Yes, even a baby whale has a guardian angel. During each activation, I cried and cried for no reason. I did not understand why. I discovered the reason the next morning before I arrived at Phuket Marine Biological Center (PMBC) that Hope had passed away during the night. So, as fate would have it, I was destined all along to work with, and look after Jamil, the baby boy Dugong.

Jamil was stranded without his mother on July 1, 2019, in Krabi, in the southern part of Thailand. He was estimated to be only three months old at the time. The marine vet theorized that a wild adult male dugong chased away the baby to mate with his mother. Usually, a baby dugong stays with their mom until 18 months old, so he was noticeably young to be away from his mother. The team of marine vets discovered that he developed signs of stress and infections when they found him. Earlier, this year another baby girl dugong, Marium, was stranded. Her condition was quite healthy. The official decided to rehabilitate her in the open sea with 24/7 care. With Jamil stranded, the team of volunteers and marine vets now split into two teams, a 4-hour drive away from each other.

When I first arrived at PMBC, I felt heaviness in the air and realized that many marine animals had died in the area. So, I activated the Enlightening Earthbound Animal Spirits energy right away to lift the feeling in the air. A new volunteer had to be quarantined for having been in contact with a disease two to three days before entering the rehabilitation pool. During the quarantine, I visited the poolside and activated the Guardian Presence energy along with Quantum Hyper Communication energy to establish a psychic connection between Jamil and me. I also activated many planetary healing energies, so I could communicate with animals and the guardian angels of animals, Gaia and the Seraphim of the ocean. Due to a lack of volunteers on rotation, I could enter the pool within 36 hours after my arrival. It was love at first sight. Jamil came to investigate me on his own and gave me a hug. This was a surprise to a vet also in the pool, waiting to teach me the ropes. He said that usually it can take many days for Jamil to be comfortable with a new volunteer.

I am an experienced scuba diver. I had been experimenting and activating energies under the sea water for almost a year at that time. The ocean is a major part of the planet, but there are not many healers who can go into the water and help heal the water and the life within. So, as a scuba diver, I am adapted to cold water. Each day, I stayed with Jamil for four to six hours at a time. This also relieved other volunteers from their duties in the water. The head of the marine vets noticed that Jamil was extremely comfortable around me. So, I asked to be with him when he received blood tests, an ultrasound, and many other procedures. I could get him to come to me, just as any cat or dog would do, by calling his name. I could take him for a swim before and after his meals. He loved to turn upside down and have me scratch his tummy. He would use his fin to hold my hand in place at times. I would visit him to give him a pat before I went to bed. Another experienced volunteer commented that she'd noticed that Jamil reacted to my voice and my hands more than to other volunteers.

On Aug 17, 2019, Marium passed away. Around 8 pm the day after Marium died, during my day five with Jamil, he developed symptoms of bloating. Being so young, he was not able to burp on his own. The vet started to give him medicine while I started adding more Aqua energies into the water. I gave him all the healing energies that I could think of. I even stayed up one night to expand the Co-Creation energies channel via Zoom. Due to the gas in his stomach, he was unable to sink underwater to sleep. He must have been so depressed being unable to sleep for at least 30 hours. I was guided by angels to hold his heart against mine, just as a mother would lull their baby to sleep. I could help Jamil to sleep for the first time during his sickness for about four hours. On Aug 23, 2019, I was in the pool with two other vets when Jamil burped as I asked him to. I knew that he understood me; the vets thought it was a mere coincidence. So, I had him burp a total of six times in a row. By then, I became known as the "Dugong Whisperer". Later, when I could talk with a sea turtle too, they changed my title to "The Sea Whisperer". By now, he had been sick for five days, and it worsened every day.

On August 24 in the early morning, I visited Jamil before my flight back to Bangkok for a business meeting. I was supposed to stay overnight in Bangkok before returning to Jamil the next day. After I said, "See you soon", he went into shock. I stayed as long as I could. While I drove to the airport, tears came from nowhere. I just knew that it was almost the end of his time on Earth. So, I prayed, and I dedicated all the good karma deeds I had done, so if he were to cross over, it would carry him to better realms and dimensions. I was told he was still hanging on when I arrived at the airport. I changed my flight right away to return to Phuket the same day. That afternoon, he was admitted for an operation in a human hospital so we could remove the indigestion that caused the bloating. After the operation, he went into another shock. One of the vets told me that Jamil hung on for an exceptionally long time. The vet really believed that Jamil was doing his best to wait for my return. However, he crossed over as I boarded the plane back. I gave him a flower before we carried him to perform a biopsy.

Until this day, anytime I do good karma, I still think of Jamil. Jamil will remain forever in my heart. It was a special ten days of my life. I am grateful for Seraphim Blueprint energies, especially Planetary Healing, Seraphim Aqua Dynamics, Guardians of Gaia, and Co-Creation with Gaia. I would not be able to have had this amazing opportunity without them. I am looking forward to other missions. One day, when I become a Seraphim Blueprint teacher, I will have many stories and experiences to share with my students. I have decided to return to PMBC every other month to work with many stranded Sea Turtles who are in rehab at the center.

Alex, a Seraphim Blueprint teacher, mentioned that he felt that Marium and Jamil are soulmates. He felt that Jamil could feel that Marium had crossed over. So, he followed. Alex mentioned that if Marium were to be within the same vicinity of Jamil, both would still be alive today. The team of marine vets also agreed with this. Marium was about to be transferred from the open sea to the rehab pool. However, due to stress, she did not last any longer for us to transport her to the pool at PMBC. Local folklore also said that if one dugong were stranded alive, his or her soulmate would follow them on land. This always happened throughout recorded history.

Since then, I began to have visions. In my dreams, I would be able to foresee the type of animal about to be stranded and which veterinarian in the Department of Marine and Coastal resources would be responsible, or where the animal would be stranded. Each time that I dreamt, I would send a message to the vet in my dream, and they turned out to be perfectly accurate. I just found out from a heart-to-heart conversation with a veterinarian who used to be based in Phuket that when she was there, she also used to have the same kind of dreams that I had. Her dreams stopped after she moved to another marine center. Did I inherit this divine gift when I arrived in Phuket? Only the angel would know for sure.

On May 23, 2020, all the dreams until now had been of a dead stranded specimen except on this day; I saw myself walking past a rehab pool in Phuket with a dolphin with black and white markings on it. June 8, 2020, I received a photo of that same dolphin just stranded a day prior and now residing in that rehab pool. I drove straight home from the gym, grabbed anything I could think of and left for Phuket right away. The vet in charge already knew of my work, so this time I entered the pool the same day that I'd arrived at the center. She showed signs of improvement, but I also sensed that she did not have the will to live. Sadly, she moved on after ten days in the pool.

Do you remember the vet who told me Jamil was hanging on for me to come back from Bangkok? He told me he often sees spirits, a male and a female. If he saw a darker skin male spirit with curly hair, an animal will die within the next 24 hours. If he saw a brighter skin lady with long black hair in a white dress, a rare marine species is bound to strand alive within the next three days. I had seen a curly-haired man with dark skin standing next to Jamil's pool one day before he passed. On Aug 11, 2020, I saw the white-dressed lady walk by, and a dolphin stranded alive a few days after. The dolphin died on its way to the center, though.

I decided to stay in Phuket to volunteer in a coral reef

restoration project at the same government facility. Corals may look like flowers and trees under the sea, but they are animals. As the storms hit, and coral bleaching occurs, the coral died. I wanted to get in the water and enlighten earth-bound animal spirits, while also sending love, and heal the water at the same time. I got to visit many other governmental marine centers, and meet and help the life of many governmental agents. The Seraph told me before I met the dugong last year that most of my new work will be with the kingdom of nature, but I still have about twenty percent of human-related work left to do. People started to call on me and my expertise to assist them, both in the water and at their centers, whenever possible.

People always asked me if and how they could live a life like I do. I always tell them that their angel, the divine, is waiting to answer their call that they are ready to help others, and only then will the angel answer and make a house call to get them to work with angels. Anything is possible. The universe is filled with infinite possibilities. Miracles and magic do exist. The angels are always there, you just have to let them in. I hope that my story inspires you to form a better relationship with your own angels and the divine, so that one day you can live an amazing life, while helping others the way I do.

Thanapon Chaivanichakul is a channeler, healer and Seraphim Blueprint practitioner. He follows earth signs, synchronicity in the universe, and the voice of the Divine to be in the right place, at the right time, to be with the people, or animals that he can assist. He also works with angels and Mother Gaia. He resides in Bangkok, Thailand.

Dragon Slayer

I was deployed on an aircraft carrier for Operation Enduring Freedom outside Iraq in 2005. I was a personnel specialist. That means I was a secretary for the Navy, and did all the paperwork for pay, and knew all the instruction manuals.

Every department had a space to maintain and clean on the ship. Well, our space needed to be spray-painted. So, we had fire-retardant brown paper that had to cover everything that didn't need to be spray-painted. As I was putting the brown paper on the wall along with someone else, I backed into a manhole. The manhole dropped at least 30 decks. On the way down, I hit the back of my head, and I swung up my left arm and grabbed the arch pipe, which saved my life. I pulled up my whole body out of the manhole. I went to Medical afterwards. I had ripped ligaments in my left shoulder when I caught the pipe.

Fast forward to the end of my career; I was stationed in Maryland at NAS Patuxent River. I was at the top of my military career. I was a Military Police Lieutenant. I was the first non-DOD police officer to be promoted to lieutenant. I broke three glass ceilings. Because I was a woman in charge of a male-dominated field, I received a lot of slack and harassment.

Besides my main job as a Police Lieutenant, I was also the fitness leader for the Security Department. It was sad because all my peers were out of shape, and I was the only soldier in outstanding fitness in the Department, so they had to promote me as the Fitness Leader.

One early morning, as I led a military workout, I felt a burning shock wave shooting down my left arm. I had to go to Medical, and when the X-rays came back, they showed that there was no spinal curvature in my neck. It was a straight line. The technician gave me a diagnosis of four herniated spinal disks.

After seven years of my initial head bang on ship, Medical declared that I couldn't arm up anymore. And since I was a Police Lt., I couldn't lead with no side arm from the front if there was an emergency. So instead of putting me in administration, they made me a sentry on gate duty. On the 13th hour of being a gate sentry and standing all night, I crumpled in front of the cars because I could not stand any more.

Being restricted to base, I had nothing else to do but to go to church, and there I made friends with the chaplain. One day back at the barracks, I dropped to my knees and said, "God if you help me, I will forever serve you."

As soon as I was allowed off base, I noticed the grass was greener, the sky bluer, and I started seeing signs that God was with me because everything in creation was talking to me. From that day forward, after seeing all the evil in the world, I decided to start studying how to fight against evil. It seemed only people of the Dark were studying the forbidden art of magic. We need more Harry Potters, and Merlins in this world.

I went to see a spiritual healer named Becky Ridgell. As I lay on her table, she did a laying on of hands. My body was trembling like a leaf. Everything was being shaken out of me. Towards the end of the session, I fell into a deep sleep. When Becky finished, she woke me. When I was half awake, I looked up and saw a silhouette of an old bearded knight sitting in her chair. It was St. George, the Dragon Slayer.

After that session with Becky, I trained with her to learn what I could. I also studied Native American religion. I studied angel healing. I became a certified Angel Practitioner. When I was ready to make business cards, I went to my other spiritual teacher, Jane Lancaster, who later became my godmother, and asked her if I should put 'house blessings' on my card. She responded, "Would you be able to go against Satan?"

"No."

"So, don't put it on your card."

I had become a spiritual seeker, and, after two years, I saw a movie called "The Conjuring". In it, a couple, Lorraine and Ed Warren, fight against evil, and are demonologists. They are the only paranormal demonologists accepted by the Catholic Church to do exorcisms besides the qualified priests. The movie "The Conjuring" is scarier than "The Exorcist". It scared me Catholic! I wanted to be protected from evil, and Catholicism was the only religion that I knew which did exorcisms. I immediately took a Catholic Conversion class. At Easter, that spring of 2015, I was baptized Catholic.

Soon thereafter, I stayed at the home of a woman named Tracy, who also wanted a healing from me. She called me in the middle of night in hysteria. Because of the hour and because I was broken-hearted over a recent family event, it was my weakest time. I lay back down. Out of nowhere a loud voice commanded, "Get up!" My body shot up from the dead and rose. It was God. I dropped back to my pillow; again, the loud voice shouted sternly, "Get up!" I arose again and said to God, "I can't". The third time the voice shouted, "Getup!" my spirit arose as from the dead miraculously, and I put my feet over the bed as my spirit had been awakened, and I found strength to put my shoes on, "Do I have to, God?" I got up and drove across the state to the client in the middle of the night. She was a lesbian who had previously been involved with a woman who was into sadomasochistic sex. The more they practiced this together, the more Tracy became a zombie with serious health issues as a result. Her ex stopped Tracy from going to church. This is how the devil can lead you astray.

I became fully involved in trying to help Tracy and rid her of all the dark energy that was in her house. We started to do a whole house cleaning to prepare for a ritual clearing, leaving nothing unturned. To begin the house clearing, I burned a bundle of sage, said Catholic house-clearing prayers and used Native American shamanism to cast out all evil spirits. Finally, I got to the basement. I worked around the whole basement until I came upon the cellar door and opened it. I smudged the sage into the back of the cellar steps. Suddenly, I became sick to my stomach. Then I saw big red eyes behind the cellar steps glaring at me. The evil creature had pointy ears and wasn't human. I was freaked out, but kept calm, as if I saw nothing. I continued to the rest of the basement saying Catholic prayers to banish evil and smudging. I went upstairs and told Tracy, "Do you realize you have something in the basement?"

Tracy then said, "I had Catholic priests here two years ago because my bed was possessed."

"Why didn't you tell me this?"

As I was staying there, I wanted both of us to stay safe from attacks. I started researching demonology to figure out how to banish this evil entity. I left to get my priest bag of tools for spiritual warfare. I then told Tracy to get her serpentine crystal ball. I taught her how to scry, using a crystal ball, and asked her, "What do you see?" She told me. I said, "Draw it for me." She used her clairvoyance and drew what she saw in the crystal ball on a notepad. And it was a dragon serpent with big pointy ears! So, now we both knew that we saw the same thing.

After a week passed, I said I must get ready for a ritual banishment. That night I started writing the plan of attack to fully banish this dragon from hell and send it back where it came from. I wrote everything out that I would be saying and doing, and prepared candles and got everything together for our protection.

I then had one dilemma, how was I going to get the dragon into the circle? I didn't know any Catholic exorcists, but I did know a pagan from the military. I contacted my friend Phil Carrol and asked him how was I going to get the dragon in the circle. He said, "Put an article of Tracy's clothing in the circle that has her smell from the past 24 hours." So, I wrote down further directions of how not to be detected by the dragon once we were outside the circle. And I was ready to go downstairs. Even though I had never done anything remotely like this, I felt confident. It was close to midnight, and I was ready to do the exorcism because I now knew how to weaken the dragon.

I started by saying, "I bless myself and Tracy as I hold a vision of my body and hers in their perfection. I call upon the green ray of healing to dissipate all areas of disharmony and bring wholeness to me and her now." I then grabbed my "protective" Navy rope to create the circle. I laid one end of the rope on the floor, and, moving clockwise, I placed the rest of the rope on the floor to form a circle. I made the circle large enough for me and Tracy to sit inside and to include my altar with candles in the center. I then took my crystal wand and went around the circle three times, envisioning the light of protection being laid down to let nothing in or out.

I then called upon divine energy, as we both stood in the protective circle.

Invocation:

"God, Archangel Michael, and your army of angels, angels of the highest vibration of love and light, please use the energy of the earth, this sage, this holy water, this Bible, these two crucifixes, and this crystal wand to remove from me any negative hooks, negative entities, attachments, soul fragments, negative karmic cords, imports, or negative thought forms. Please remove them in full power now, and fill and heal the space with white light and St. Germaine's violet flame of love and positivity. Please return any negative entities and demons or energies to the light and surround me and those with me, including Tracy's pets, with your divine protection now and always. Please create a shield of angels to work on my behalf to keep me clear and in the light in a way that is with ease and grace. Thank you. It is done, it is done, and it is done. Blessed be."

We both sat down and meditated for ten minutes for

everything to set in place. I rose and told Tracy to stand. I took my wand and went into the circle and put a circle of light to shield us and blind us out of sight of the dragon so he wouldn't see us leave the circle. We both stepped out of the circle facing north. I opened the circle to the west. I threw in Tracy's pair of boxers with her smell on them. I said, "Go and get her." The dragon shadow went in the circle, and I immediately closed the rope circle behind the dragon. I gave Tracy holy water and a wooden crucifix while I said: "In the name of the Holy Father, Son and Holy Spirit", and while I held a crucifix made of olive wood from Jerusalem, I read from my 150-year-old leather palm Bible handed down to me from a Knight of Columbus who was my second cousin. Then we waited for all the forces inside to beat that dragon trapped in the circle.

The candles inside the circle were doing miraculous things. Two of the candles were melting together and forming a shape. This I recognized as it was releasing the binding spell that a gypsy had bound Tracy with her ex, a demi-demon in a twin-flame love spell to be together forever. That was broken. We sat there for hours watching the candles melt in ways that were unnatural and spectacular. We stayed there all night to make sure that the black protection against evil was completely gone. Then I would know for certain the dragon from hell was banished and extinguished.

The dragon was trapped in the Black Candle against evil. The black candle in the glass was almost burnt out. It had a fraction of black wax on the bottom. It then came to me to get the Catholic Exorcism Rite. I grabbed the rite of paper of exorcism in Latin I'd written that night while I was putting the ritual together. I read it out loud in my commanding military voice. This is the Latin Exorcism Rite:

Exorcizamuste te, omnis immunde spiritus, omni satanica potestas, omnis incursio infernalis adversarii, omnis legio, omnis congregatio et secta diabolica, in nomini et virtute Domini nostri Jesu Christi, eradicare et effugare a Dei Ecclesia, ab animabus ad imaginem. Dei conditis ac pretioso divini Agni sanguini redemptis.

Crux sacra sit mihi lux! Nunquam draco sit mihi dux. Vade retro Santana! Nunquam suade mihi vana! Sunt mala quae lbse. lpse venena bibas!

A power of the Gods came through me as I recited the incantation, which is heavily charged with energy that comes not from the mind, but from the Glory of the Gods above. I spoke with deep conviction. I told Tracy to keep putting her cross back and forth toward the dragon as I said the incantation with power and precise pronunciation. I, too, was holding my cross in my right hand and the paper in my left with the old Bible facing forward to the dragon. Flames of the Corner Animal candle were shooting in the air and into the glass black candle where the dragon had been sucked in. Each time I spoke Latin loudly, flames were arching into the black candle of evil and burning the dragon from hell. I felt a big charge of energy shoot down through me from the heavens as I was giving all that I had as an elite military warrior. I couldn't explain the immensity of power that was coming out of me.

In the fifteen minutes of saying the incantation repeatedly, the dragon was trying to pull the crucifix out of my hands. I had to use all my might. The knuckles of my hands were even turning white as the dragon's force was pulling so hard and my hands were getting sweaty. I looked at my hand and squeezed with all I had. He's not going to win. I then looked down and saw my white crystal wand pointing straight at the Black Candle Jar to where the dragon was inside and saw it glowing with white light shooting at the dragon. Jesus and God had light and all the forces above shooting white light into my wand pointing at the Dragon. This was better than the Merlin stories I'd read, or Harry Potter, for that matter. This was the real deal.

After thirty minutes of shouting in a deep, military voice, I started to get out of breath, as all the forces of good and the power that was coming out of me were beyond any force imaginable. The flames continued to arch and send the dragon to hell with each fire-spit that came off my golden tongue of fire until there was no more wax, or candle, or dragon inside the candle.

We looked at each other in such relief. Then the brightest light came from the ceiling, and we couldn't see in the middle because the light was that bright. Jesus Christ came out of the bright light. Tracy exclaimed, "My Lord!"

I sat down on the cellar step in awe. I said to her in a loud voice, "Repent! Take all your memories of sadomasochistic torture and give them to the Lord to erase." She got on her knees and pleaded with God. As she looked up into the bright light that was as bright as the sun beams around Jesus, she repented and cried as she was pleading to the Lord. I sat as St. George the Dragon Slayer took over my body, and I felt his presence as I just nodded and looked down as a Knight, "I serve the Lord as my chief commander." And I was at rest because I felt his Knightly presence taking over me humbly and with great valor. She continued to cry and repent. I was sitting on the cellar step looking down because his light was so great, and, cautiously, I would look at her and see what she was doing repenting. I could hardly look at Him because Christ was so magnificent. I could do nothing but serve my King and bow before Him. When the repenting was done, the Light and Jesus began to disappear. Tracy stayed on her knees crying. I got up and asked her if she had given up all her evil memories of her ex? And she said, "Yes".

The banishment of the Dragon from Hell was complete, and the ceremony was finally over. It was a long, timeless night.

Tracy started to get tired, so she lay down to go to sleep. Tracy had only lain down for approximately fifteen minutes when, suddenly, she popped up as if rising from the dead. I watched her body. The right side of the zombie disfigurement she had was popped into place. Her left shoulder that was limp was no longer limp and hanging forward; it was evened out with the left side of her body. I watched as her spine also cracked into place. And her head rose as everything was set into place. I could not do what Jesus Christ can do by far because he is the Master Healer.

A bit later, I went to the Spiritual Store and asked the lady that worked there and who had done house blessings for thirty years, "Did you ever cross a Dragon from Hell in your house blessings?

She said, "No."

I walked away and pondered, "How can I do a house blessing for the first time, and face a dragon from hell? What are the odds of that?" My godmother Jane Lancaster was right. Do not put 'house blessings' on your business card.

My best friend's father was a collector of antiques. His house looked like the TV show "American Pickers" because he had stuff everywhere. It was a little bit of a hoarder's house, but it was all valuable. As I came down the steps, he had framed an old tapestry. It was exactly what I had slain five years earlier, depicted on a biblical tapestry: a dragon's head with a serpent's body and no feet. I then realized that I had banished Satan himself. And here my godmother said, "Would you be able to fight Satan himself?" And I did. I was like Holy Shit! My mind and heart went for loops. It wasn't just a Dragon creature from Hell, it was Satan. I had always pictured Satan as depicted on the Archangel's Prayer Card, as a bull with horns. I didn't know that he could also be a Dragon. And then I remembered from Genesis how God cursed Satan:

"So, the Lord God said to the serpent, 'Because you have done this, you are cursed more than all cattle, and more than every beast of the field; on your belly you shall go, and you shall eat dust all the days of your life...'"

I, a non-Catholic priest, a commoner, who had been baptized Catholic six months earlier, had just slain Satan! Plus, Catholic priests had come two years prior to Tracey's home, and didn't do the job. I don't know what I felt, but all I can say is I love God so much and would do anything for Him who saved my life out at sea. Thus, I paid my debt to God.

Maria Sherwood transitioned out of military service and has now embraced a spiritual process of being transformed into a new identity, turning her life over completely to God. She has become transformed and remolded, as clay in God's hands. All her battles are geared to being a true Knight—a Dragon Slayer.

A Strange Encounter

Sometimes we receive unexpected guidance in unexpected places and at unexpected times. One of my strangest encounters happened in 1990 while on vacation during a 50-mile backpacking trip in the great Smoky Mountain National Park. I had looked forward to this trip for about a year and had planned to be walking along the Appalachian Trail in Tennessee when the Rhododendrons would be in full bloom. On my first day, I would have to hike about 16 miles, starting from a trail-head, walking through a forest and then up a mountain to get to the main Appalachian Trail that ran along the top of a ridge. That first night, I planned to stay in a park shelter.

I picked a gorgeous day to start my backpacking trip. The weather was beautiful, the forest was green and lush and the air was crisp, clean, humid, and filled with a heavy scent of wild flowers. About eight miles or so into the forest, I suddenly realized that there wasn't another soul around for miles. Here, I could finally relax, let my guard down and enjoy the natural beauty around me. At that moment, I felt the presence of the Being of Nature, and then an amazing feeling of peace and tranquility flooded my awareness, and my heart was filled with joy. I walked a little bit longer through what now seemed like a magical playground because everything seemed so bright and beautiful. All my senses were fully opened and greatly amplified. A little bit further, the forest opened into a meadow filled with wild flowers and grass. After walking through it, I noticed that the trail would now be going up a steep mountain, so I decided that this would be a good time to take a quick breather before I began my ascent. Looking for a place to sit next to the trail at the edge of the meadow, I noticed that several logs had already been arranged into a bench—a perfect rest spot.

As soon as I sat down, I couldn't help but notice how connected I felt to everything around me and how beautiful this place was. My mind was at peace. And then, I heard startling noises coming from the forest ahead that sounded like boulders crashing down the mountainside and trees falling over. Something was coming toward me, and it was getting closer and louder. However, I'm not sure if it was really that loud, or if it just seemed loud because all my senses were in a heightened state of awareness. Whatever the case, it was disturbing my inner Zen like throwing pebbles into a still pond and creating waves that spread out in every direction.

At last, coming out of the forest was a man who had been running down the trail. He saw me sitting there and asked if it would be all right for him to sit a few minutes. I nodded, "Yes," and with an open hand gesture waved him to the log next to mine.

So, there we were, two strangers sitting on a log, deep in the wilderness, miles away from civilization or any other people and just started to have this amazing conversation about life that went on nonstop for about two hours. What was also odd is that I never thought of asking for his name, nor did he ask for mine. That just didn't seem important. I can't explain it, but it was as if I already knew him. I felt comfortable in his presence, and so it was easy to talk about everything that came to mind because I knew I wouldn't be judged. It was as if he was an old soul, and even though he physically appeared to be in his early thirties, his deep inner wisdom, gentle kindness of heart, and presence of Being, reminded me of a grandfather figure. There was a lot I could learn from him, and it felt as if I had several thousand years of catching up to do.

We talked about modern medicine and its inadequacy, alternative forms of healing that included nutrition, herbs, and energy medicine, as well as various metaphysical topics. Our conversation went back-and-forth, as we shared ideas and what we'd learned, essentially comparing our notes on life. Some of his ideas were so radical, that I could hardly wrap my mind around them because I would have never thought of them on my own, so he would expound upon them to tweak my thinking so I could now understand. And the ideas that I came up with and shared served as a foundation onto which he showed me how to build something better. Within that short, but intense two hours, I felt that I had learned more than my previous ten years. I had so many new ideas, thought patterns, and concepts dancing around in my mind, like little balls of light colliding into each other, that I felt overwhelmed. My brain now needed time to process every-thing before I could fully make sense of it all.

Over the course of our conversation, I recall that the stranger had repeatedly, at least five times, suggested and encouraged me to write a book. But, I was thinking all along to myself that I am not a writer; I'm not talented in that way; so how could I possibly write a book? Besides, I didn't have the time. And then, as if he could read my mind and sense my doubts, he said, being a little more direct this time, "Just start writing."

I responded with, "Since most of these ideas are yours, why don't you write a book?" He never did answer my question; however, he did give me further encouragement by telling me that my books will be great.

So, it came time for us to part ways. We both stood up. I put my backpack on, but, oddly, he wasn't carrying anything. I thanked him for everything. He turned to walk down the trail, and I turned up the trail. I took two steps, stopped, and turned back around to thank him again and wish him well. But he was gone. Where did he go? I looked down the trail and ahead into the meadow below, but he wasn't there. The meadow was 30-35 yards across, and it just didn't seem possible that anybody could make it all the way through so quickly. I stood there confused. I looked around the forest a little bit more, thinking he went off trail, but he was nowhere to be found. And then, as if someone sensed my confusion, I heard loud noises coming from the forest below that sounded just like what I heard earlier announcing his arrival: boulders crashing down the mountainside and trees falling over. In my mind, I immediately rationalized that the noises were from him running through the forest and that he must have been fast crossing the meadow. I could now let it go and move on. However, later, during my hike, my unanswered question resurfaced. But this time, to resolve the confusion, I calculated that the time it took for me to take two steps and turn around, which was the time he was out of sight, was about two seconds. There is no way it was humanly possible for the stranger to have gotten across the meadow so quickly. Who was this guy?

Today, in writing this story, some thirty years after my encounter with that stranger deep in the forest, most of the details of what we had talked about have faded away, have become irrelevant, or simply have merged into my own thoughts, in which I no longer remember exactly whose thoughts were whose. But, more importantly, what has remained over the years are new thinking patterns and concepts that I had first acquired in my talk with the stranger.

If you change the way you think, you change the structure of your brain. Science tells us that if you acquire a new thinking pattern, new neural circuits will form in your brain. And, according to the concept of neuroplasticity, the more you think a certain way, the stronger and more developed its associated neural pathways in your brain become, essentially crystallizing the new energy pattern into the physical realm. I believe that the conversation I had with that stranger so many years ago not only changed my thinking patterns, and consequently my brain, but in doing so, it has continued to shape, influence, and define my life even today.

Looking back over the years, I have come to realize that the stranger had set things in motion, causing a sequence of events to occur that probably would not have happened on their own. He changed the way I think, and in doing so, he changed the trajectory of my life. When I first met the stranger, it was as a research scientist, then years later, I became a professor, and then more recently, I was inspired to become a spiritual teacher and healer. With each career change, there were key things learned and skills acquired laid the foundation and created the possibility for the next career step. I'm not sure where all of this is heading, but I really like all the changes so far. My field of happiness has grown by leaps and bounds because I have learned how to get my life better aligned with the original possibilities first presented to me by the stranger so many years ago. I can hardly wait to see what happens next.

I wonder how much that happens in our lives can be traced back to a single seed thought from an inspiration, a conversation, or an event that happened years earlier. I suspect that if you really look closely at your life, you will discover, as I have with mine, that almost everything happening in your life today can be traced back to single seed thoughts from years ago, thoughts that changed your thinking patterns. Changing the way you think will create new possibilities for your life.

Who was the stranger? Returning to my earlier question on *who was this guy*, I came up with several possibilities. My first thought was that he was a man, albeit brilliant, but I ruled this out because it was not humanly possible for anyone to disappear or get across the meadow so quickly. Next, I entertained the possibility that he was a ghost. After all, in the forest on the trail that day, I was experiencing a heightened state of awareness with celestial perception. Also, considering that I never actually shook hands with him or touched the stranger, as far as I knew, I could have been talking to a ghost. But, I ruled out this possibility because independent earthbound souls (ghosts) do not have access to the fifth dimensional realm and its infinite resource of information. Earthbound souls only have the knowledge that they acquired during their recent life on earth. The person I talked to on the trail that day had a depth of knowledge, understanding and wisdom that seemed to span time itself, the likes of which I have never experienced before. Furthermore, ghosts usually do not have the power to move boulders or knock over trees as this Being had in announcing his arrival. Who was this guy?

My next consideration was an angel. Angels are messengers of God, so it would make sense that this person was an angelic being. Historically, angels have served as spirit guides, protectors, messengers, guardians and healers. Angels can take on human form when needed. There are countless examples of Divine intervention by angels. For example, Mohammed, a prophet of God, over the course of twenty-three years, received revelations from God through the Archangel Gabriel for writing the Quran.

Since that encounter with the stranger so many years ago, I have acquired various types of spiritual tools and abilities. Using my skills, and connecting with Divine Source, I started asking questions. I could rule out that the stranger was an angel, archangel, or any other commonly known types of angelic beings. All I found out was that the stranger was a "Being of Light" who was sent to guide me. That was it. What I knew for sure is that his guidance from so many years ago had changed and redirected my life into what it is today. For this, I owe him my gratitude. To get more details about him, I had to turn to someone more skilled in these matters, so I consulted a psychic who was gifted at communicating with angels and spirit guides. If anyone could find out, it would be this psychic.

With the psychic's help, I got a clearer picture of what

really happened back then, and now for the first time, it's starting to make sense. The stranger I encountered so many years ago turned out to be Zedmiel, a "Being of Light" from the Leo Galaxy. He is one of God's special spiritual guides of the universe. His visit was God's gift for giving me different directions and possibilities in my life. I was also told that it is extremely rare for anyone to see Zedmiel, especially in the way he chose to meet with me. I suspect that I am somewhat dense, and so, Zedmiel knew that he would have to use a direct approach and come down to this physical realm to create new possibilities in my life.

In my opinion, Zedmiel's cosmic role is much like that of a gardener who plants different kinds of seeds in the soil. Not all the seeds will germinate. But, those that do are given water and fertilizer to keep them growing. Sometimes the gardener might have to plant new seeds to replace those that failed to grow.

In a similar way, Zedmiel planted seed thoughts of new possibilities in my mind. Not all these seeds germinated. Some resonated with me better than others. Since I have a free will, I could choose which of these new ideas, concepts and thinking patterns to adopt in my life. The psychic had told me that Zedmiel had watched over me for the rest of my backpacking trip and had given me several re-installations of his seed thoughts. I do recall, on several occasions while hiking, having a sudden obsession to go over in my mind about the conversation I had earlier with Zedmiel, and just like before, I had the sensation of little balls of light bouncing around in my mind and colliding with each other. There was so much new information given to me, that my biggest concern was that I wouldn't be able to remember it all. I had no pen or paper to write these ideas down, and so I had to rely on my memory. By the time I completed my trip five days later, I had already forgotten much of what we had talked about. But, it really didn't matter that I forgot the details. Only the seed thoughts I'd acquired were important. Not all of them were meant to be retained. The only seed thoughts that persisted were those that resonated with me, and on a deep subconscious level, I chose to give them the opportunity to germinate and reach fruition in my life.

I learned that Zedmiel, like a good gardener checking on his plants, occasionally checks in on me from time to time to see how I am doing and give me additional insights or direction if needed. He comes to me while I am either in deep meditation or sleeping at night when on a higher astral plane, and so, I am not consciously aware or remember when he visits. I suspect that like a gardener adding extra fertilizer, his occasional input from behind the scenes in bringing key people and the right circumstances into my life over the years has created the fertile ground necessary for the continued growth and fruition of the seed thoughts he had originally given me. What a blessing Zedmiel has been to my life.

I also got clarification about the loud noises I heard coming from the forest that started with a loud boom followed by sounds of boulders crashing down the mountainside and trees falling over, announcing Zedmiel's arrival. I was told that they were the result of Zedmiel coming down to Earth. His energy field is so large and powerful that he had difficulty compressing it down in size. So, when he first landed on the trail, his energy field was still too large, and it extended out beyond the sides of the trail. It was so powerful that it knocked over trees and pushed boulders aside. Oops! By the time Zedmiel had reached me further down the trail and came out of the forest, he had just finished compressing his energy field into a physical form.

I can confirm that there was damage to the forest. After my conversation with Zedmiel ended and as I walked away and up the trail, I saw trees on either side had been knocked over. The further up the trail I went, the more trees had been damaged. And then, about a quarter of a mile up the trail, I came to a spot where there had been massive damage to the forest. Lots of trees on either side had been pushed down and away from the trail. I had never seen anything like it, and at that time, I had no explanation of what could cause so much damage. Perhaps there had been an avalanche from the previous winter, but there was no sign of an avalanche shoot coming down the mountainside. Perhaps forest rangers were in the process of clearing out this area, but the trees were not cut, they were snapped apart or bent. Standing on the trail, at the center of the damage, I could see that the snapped trees spread out like spokes of a wheel. The trees closest to the center were snapped at their base; further out, they were snapped higher and higher up the tree. At the perimeter, only the very tops of the trees had been damaged. How strange. I recall that back then, I had even momentarily entertained the idea that a giant ball, which must have been several hundred feet in diameter, had fallen from the sky onto the trail, pushing everything out of its way and creating this circular pattern of destruction. I quickly dismissed that idea because that would be crazy, right? Down the trail from this spot to where I had been sitting, the physical damage to the forest tapered off. Up the trail from this spot, there was no further sign of damage. I now believe that the pattern of destruction to the forest I had witnessed years ago is consistent with what was described by the psychic about the circumstances behind Zedmiel's arrival. In my wildest dreams, I would have never imagined anything as incredible as this. This truly was a strange encounter.

If Zedmiel is aware of what I have written here, I would like first and foremost to express my gratitude for all your help. Second, please visit Earth more often. No disrespect intended, but obviously, you need practice with your landings and take-offs. May I suggest that you try landing in an open field to minimize damage? We do love our trees.

Eugene Nau has a PhD in biology. He has many years of teaching experience that encompass both natural sciences and healing modalities. He had been a research scientist, an assistant professor, and now a dedicated healer helping others. He resides in Cheyenne, Wyoming, and teaches Seraphim Blueprint workshops in person, or by teleconference.

The 2023 Seraphic Prize

In November of 2023, the third Seraphic Prize will be awarded to members of the public who compose the best spiritual short story (fictional account), or non-fiction account, with the optional mention of angels. Seraphim Alliance will then publish a collection of up to fifteen stories in a volume to be published in 2024.

Individual entries are limited to 3,333 words, which is a little more than thirteen pages, of 250 words per page.

- The 2023 Seraphic Prize will be likely be awarded in mid-December.
- First prize is $1,000, plus publication
- Second prize is $500, plus publication
- Third-place prize is to be shared by thirteen authors whose work will appear in the volume to be published in 2024.
- Please send inquiries and entries to Ruth Rendely (info@seraphimblueprint.org)
- All entries must be received by midnight August 31, 2023.

What is Seraphim Blueprint?

Thirteen thousand years ago a group of high angels called Seraphim created a cosmology that humanity could use for its well-being and evolution. Atlantean priests first cognized this system. Then the early Hebrews re-cognized these energies and created the Kabbalah. In modern times the energies resurfaced in 1994 when a Seraph contacted Ruth Rendely, a meditation instructor.

Seraphim Blueprint is a cosmological collection of energies that are permanently stored in the ethers. The Seraphim that created this system chose to give out these energies in a specific sequence that harmoniously integrates with our nervous systems.

The system includes eleven major energies that synergistically interact to enhance our life-force energy and well-being. Each major energy, or waveform, has its own purpose and distinct quality that provides a unique evolutionary pathway for Self-Realization.

The energies are safe and intelligent and are pre-programmed to ideally adapt to our unique life situation and physical condition. They work on all levels of our physical, emotional, mental and spiritual bodies.

www.SeraphimBlueprint.com

Worldwide Courses

Seraphim Blueprint training is now available on five continents, including North America, Europe, Africa, Asia and Australia. To find a Teacher in your location, please go to the teachers' page on the SeraphimBlueprint.org website. The Seraphim Blueprint Levels are taken in sequence, starting with Seraphim Healing. These angelic initiations are facilitated in one or two-day workshops, either by a teacher who is personally present, or long distance via conference calls, or through the Internet. Even if you live in a remote rural area, you will be able to receive these energies worldwide if you have access to these forms of communication. Currently, Ruth and about one hundred and fifty teachers facilitate these workshops. To find out more about the courses available to you and the fees involved, please contact individual teachers.